THIRD EDITION

WORLD**LINK**

Developing
English Fluency

Level 1

Nancy Douglas

James R. Morgan

**NATIONAL
GEOGRAPHIC
LEARNING**

CENGAGE
Learning·

Australia • Brazil • Mexico • Singapore • United Kingdom • United States

World Link Level 1: Developing English Fluency, Third Edition

Nancy Douglas, Author

James R. Morgan, Author

Susan Stempleski, Series Editor

Publisher: Sherrise Roehr

Executive Editor: Sarah Kenney

Development Editor: Brenden Layte

Associate Development Editor: Alison Bruno

Assistant Editor: Patricia Giunta

Media Researcher: Leila Hishmeh

Senior Technology Product Manager:
  Lauren Krolick

Director of Global Marketing: Ian Martin

Senior Product Marketing Manager:
  Caitlin Thomas

Sr. Director, ELT & World Languages:
  Michael Burggren

Production Manager: Daisy Sosa

Content Project Manager: Beth Houston

Senior Print Buyer: Mary Beth Hennebury

Composition: Lumina

Cover/Text Design: Brenda Carmichael

Art Director: Brenda Carmichael

Cover Image: Eduardo Kobra

Inside Front Cover Image: AFP/Getty Images

Photo Credits are listed on the inside
  back cover.

For product information and technology assistance, contact us at
Cengage Learning Customer & Sales Support, 1-800-354-9706
For permission to use material from this text or product,
submit all requests online at **www.cengage.com/permissions**
Further permissions questions can be emailed to
permissionrequest@cengage.com

World Link 1 ISBN: 978-1-305-65078-7

World Link 1 + My World Link Online ISBN: 978-1-305-65079-4

National Geographic Learning
20 Channel Center Street
Boston, MA 02210
USA

Cengage Learning is a leading provider of customized learning solutions with employees residing in nearly 40 different countries and sales in more than 125 countries around the world. Find your local representative at **www.cengage.com**

Cengage Learning products are represented in Canada by Nelson Education, Ltd.

Visit National Geographic Learning online at ngl.cengage.com
Visit our corporate website at **cengage.com**

Printed in China by RRD
Print Number: 08   Print Year: 2020

Acknowledgments

We would like to extend a very special thank you to the Instituto Cultural Peruano Norteamericano (ICPNA) academic management staff in the central office, branches and teachers, for the helpful insights and suggestions that contributed toward the development of this series.

We would also like to thank Raúl Billini, English Coordinator, Mi Colegio, Dominican Republic, for his contributions to this series.

Thank you to the educators who provided invaluable feedback throughout the development of the *World Link* series: Rocio Abarca, Instituto Tecnológico de Costa Rica / FUNDATEC; David Aduviri, CBA (Centro Boliviano Americano) - La Paz; Ramon Aguilar, Universidad Tecnológica de Hermosillo; Miguel Arrazola, CBA (Centro Boliviano Americano) - Santa Cruz; Cecilia Avila, Universidad de Xalapa; Isabel Baracat, CCI (Centro de Comunicação Inglesa); Daniel Sanchez Bedoy, Calfornia Language Center; Andrea Brotto, CEICOM (Centro de Idiomas para Comunidades); George Bozanich, Soongsil University; Emma Campo, Universidad Central; Andrea Carlson, Aichi Prefectural University; Martha Carrasco, Universidad Autonoma de Sinaloa; Herbert Chavel, Korea Advanced Institute of Science and Technology; J. Ventura Chavez, Universidad de Guadalajara CUSUR; Denise de Bartolomeo, AMICANA (Asociación Mendocina de Intercambio Cultural Argentino Norteamericano); Rodrigo de Campos Rezende, SEVEN Idiomas; John Dennis, Hokuriku University; Kirvin Andrew Dyer, Yan Ping High School; Marilena Fernandes, Alumni; Mark Firth, J.F. Oberlin University; Daniela Frillochi, ARICANA (Asociación Rosarina de Intercambio Cultural Argentino Norteamericano); Joseph Gabriella, Toyo University; Marina Gonzalez, Instituto Universitario de Lenguas Modernas; Robert Gordon, Korea Advanced Institute of Science and Technology; Scott Grigas, Youngsan University; Gu Yingruo, Research Institute of Xiangzhou District, ZhuHai; Kyle Hammel, Incheon National University; Mariana Gil Hammer, Instituto Cultural Dominico Americano; Helen Hanae, Toyo University; Xu Heng, Nantong Polytechnic College; Amiris Helena, Centro Cultural Dominico Americano; Rafael Hernandez, Centro Educacional Tlaquepaque; Yo-Tien Ho, Takming University; Marie Igwe, Hanseo University; Roxana Jimenez, Instituto Tecnológico de Costa Rica / FUNDATEC; Liu Jing, Shanghai Foreign Language Education Press; Lâm Nguyễn Huỳnh, Van Lang University; Hui-Chuan Liao, National Kaohsiung University of Applied Sciences; Pan Lang, Nanjing Sport Institute; Sirina Kainongsuang, Perfect Publishing Company Limited; Karen Ko, ChinYi University; Ching-Hua Lin, National Taiwan University of Science and Technology; Simon Liu, ChinYi University; Maria Helena Luna, Tronwell; Ady Marrero, Alianza Cultural Uruguay Estados Unidos; Nancy Mcaleer, ELC Universidad Interamericana de Panama, Michael McCallister, Feng Chia University Language Center; Jose Antonio Mendes Lopes, ICBEU (Instituto Cultural Brasil Estados Unidos); Tania Molina, Instituto Tecnológico de Costa Rica / FUNDATEC; Iliana Mora, Instituto Tecnológico de Costa Rica / FUNDATEC; Fernando Morales, Universidad Tecnológica de Hermosillo; Vivian Morghen, ICANA (Instituto Cultural Argentino Norteamericano); Aree Na Nan, Chiang Mai University; He Ning, Nanjing Mochou Vocational School; Paul Nugent, Kkottongnae University; Niu Yuchun, New Oriental School Beijing; Elizabeth Ortiz, COPEI (Copol English Institute); Virginia Ortiz, Universidad Autonoma de Tamaulipas; Marshall Presnick, Language Link Vietnam; Justin Prock, Pyeongtaek University; Peter Reilly, Universidad Bonaterra; Ren Huijun, New Oriental School Hangzhou; Andreina Romero, URBE (Universidad Rafael Belloso Chacín); Leon Rose, Jeonju University; Chris Ruddenklau, Kinki University; Adelina Ruiz, Instituto Tecnologico de Estudios Superiores de Occidente; Eleonora Salas, IICANA (Instituto de Intercambio Cultural Argentino Norteamericano); Jose Salas, Universidad Tecnológica del Norte de Guanajuato; Mary Sarawit, Naresuan University International College; Jenay Seymour, Hong-ik University; Huang Shuang, Shanghai International Studies University; Sávio Siqueira, ACBEU (Asociação Cultural Brasil Estados Unidos) / UFBA (Universidade Federal da Bahia); Beatriz Solina, ARICANA (Asociación Rosarina de Intercambio Cultural Argentino Norteamericano); Mari Cruz Suárez, Servicio de Idiomas UAM; Bambang Sujianto, Intensive English Course (IEC); Howard Tarnoff, Health Sciences University of Hokkaido; Emily J. Thomas, Incheon National University; Sandrine Ting, St. John's University; Tran Nguyen Hoai Chi, Vietnam USA Society English Training Service Center; Ruth Tun, Universidad Autonoma de Campeche; Rubén Uceta, Centro Cultural Dominico Americano; Maria Inés Valsecchi, Universidad Nacional de Río Cuarto; Alicia Vazquez, Instituto Internacional; Patricia Veciño, ICANA (Instituto Cultural Argentino Norteamericano); Punchalee Wasanasomsithi, Chulalongkorn University; Tomoe Watanabe, Hiroshima City University; Dhunyawat Treenate, Rajamangala University of Technology Krungthep; Haibo Wei, Nantong Agricultural College; Tomohiro Yanagi, Chubu University; Jia Yuan, Global IELTS School; Selestin Zainuddin, LBPP-LIA.

SCOPE & SEQUENCE

Grammar	Pronunciation	Speaking	Reading	Writing	Communication
Review of the simple present tense pp. 8, 195 Describing appearance using *be / have* pp. 14, 196	Question intonation review p. 6	Introducing yourself; Asking about occupations p. 7	Celebrity doubles p. 12 Skim for gist Scan for details	Describe a classmate p. 14	Ask questions to find classmates with various interests p. 9 Describe a person p. 15
Review of the present continuous tense pp. 22, 197 Subject and object pronouns pp. 28, 198	Listening for contractions p. 20	Greeting people and asking how they are p. 21	World greetings p. 26 Preview the reading Make predictions Scan for details Read for details	Write a text message p. 28	Draw a place your partner describes p. 23 Act out and guess actions p. 29
Count and noncount nouns pp. 36, 199 Quantifiers with affirmative and negative statements pp. 42, 200	Syllables p. 34	Talking about things you need p. 35	On sale in Seoul p. 40 Make predictions Identify main ideas Scan for details	Write about your favorite place to shop p. 42	Choose items to take on an island survival trip p. 37 List items a person needs and say where to buy them p. 43
Connecting ideas with *but, or,* and *so* pp. 54, 201 Possessive adjectives; possessive pronouns; *belong to* pp. 60, 202	Stress in multi-syllable words p. 52	Giving advice p. 53	How to pack for your next trip p. 58 Understand the gist Make predictions Identify main ideas Scan for details	Write about a traveling experience p. 60	Ask questions and pick a vacation destination for a partner p. 55 Ask questions about a partner's vacation p. 61
The simple past tense with *be* pp. 68, 203 The simple past: affirmative and negative statements pp. 74, 204	Past tense *-ed* endings p. 74	Agreeing or disagreeing with an opinion p. 67	Eco-fuel Africa p. 72 Make predictions Infer information Sequence events Read for details	Write about a personal hero p. 75	Plan a party and invite famous people p. 69 Discuss who should be given an award for being a hero p. 75
The simple past: affirmative and negative statements (irregular verbs) pp. 82, 205 The simple past tense: question forms pp. 88, 206	Irregular past tense verbs p. 82	Expressing degrees of certainty p. 81	A study of sleep p. 86 Identify the main idea Scan for details	Write about your sleep patterns p. 89	Recall and share childhood memories p. 83 Ask and answer questions about sleep patterns p. 89

PEOPLE

UNIT GOALS

1 Ask questions to get basic personal information

2 Introduce yourself

3 Talk about where you come from and what you do

4 Describe a person's appearance

People look at an art exhibition in Santiago de Compostela, Spain.

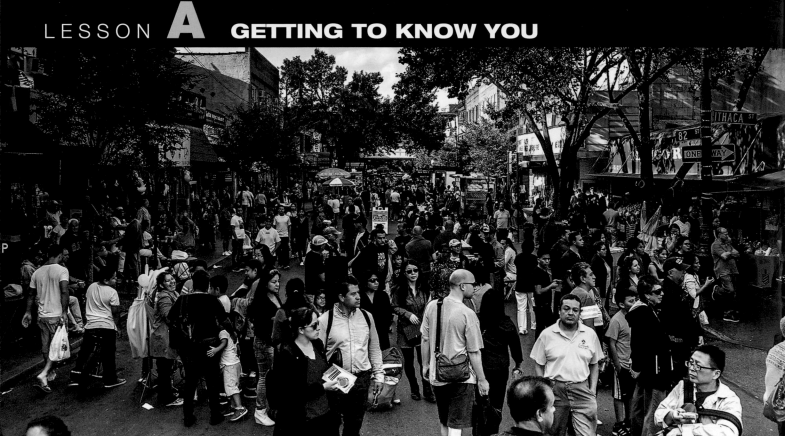

People on a busy street in New York City

1 **VIDEO** World's Biggest Melting Pot

A 🔁 Look at the photo of New York City. What do you notice about it? Tell a partner.

B ▶ Watch the video. Circle your answers.

1. Welcome to Brooklyn / Queens New York.

2. Almost half the people here were born in New York / another country.

3. They speak almost 50 / 150 languages.

ℹ️ *half = 50%*

C ▶ Watch the video again. Complete the sentences.

1. "I'm from Madras, the southern part of India. My _____ live there and my grandparents live there."

2. "My mom's from South Korea and on my father's side I am _____, Irish, English..."

3. "So you have Eastern Europeans. You have Hispanics. You have _____. You have Arabic. I like that."

D 🔁 Is your city similar to or different from this neighborhood? Use your answers in **B** and **C** to explain to a partner.

2 VOCABULARY

A Look at Silvia's LinkBook page. Do you have a page like this?

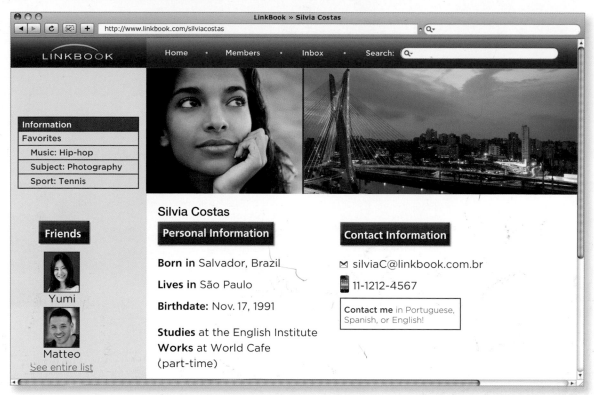

LinkBook » Silvia Costas

http://www.linkbook.com/silviacostas

LINKBOOK

Home • Members • Inbox • Search:

Information

Favorites

Music: Hip-hop

Subject: Photography

Sport: Tennis

Friends

Yumi

Matteo

See entire list

Silvia Costas

Personal Information

Born in Salvador, Brazil

Lives in São Paulo

Birthdate: Nov. 17, 1991

Studies at the English Institute
Works at World Cafe
(part-time)

Contact Information

✉ silviaC@linkbook.com.br

📱 11-1212-4567

Contact me in Portuguese, Spanish, or English!

ℹ️ **Saying email addresses**

silviaC@linkbook .com.br = silvia C (at) linkbook (dot) com (dot) b-r

B 🔁 Look at Silvia's web page. Complete the questions and answers with a partner. Use the words in the box.

born	city	first name	hometown	job	last name
phone	email address	friends	interested in	languages	subject

1. What's your ___Name___?   (It's) Silvia.
2. What's your _last name_?   (It's) Costas.
3. Where were you born?   I was _____ in Salvador. It's my _____.
4. Where do you live now?   São Paulo. It's a fun _____!
5. What do you do for fun?   I'm in a band with my _____, Yumi and Matteo.
6. What's your favorite _subject_?   I'm _____ photography.
7. How many _languages_ do you speak?   Three. I speak Portuguese, Spanish, and English.
8. What's your _email addres_?   (It's) silviaC@linkbook.com.br.
9. What's your _Phone_ number?   (It's) 11-1212-4567.
10. What do you do?   I'm a student, and I have a part-time _at Wdbl Cafe_.

C 🔁 Use the questions in **B** to interview your partner.

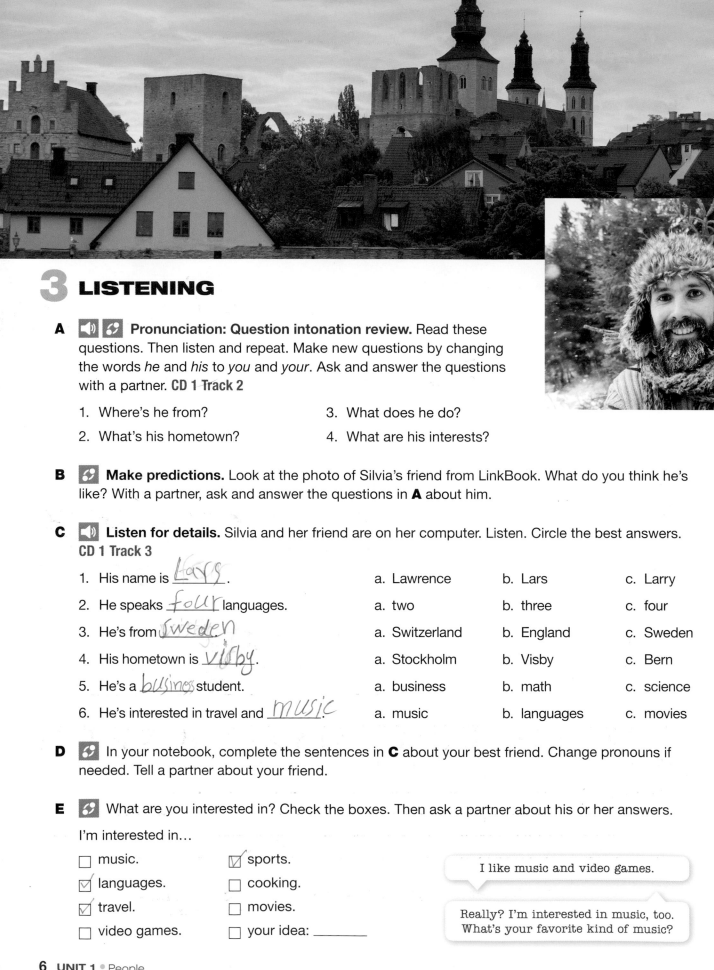

3 LISTENING

A 🔊 ⟳ **Pronunciation: Question intonation review.** Read these questions. Then listen and repeat. Make new questions by changing the words *he* and *his* to *you* and *your*. Ask and answer the questions with a partner. **CD 1 Track 2**

1. Where's he from?
2. What's his hometown?
3. What does he do?
4. What are his interests?

B ⟳ **Make predictions.** Look at the photo of Silvia's friend from LinkBook. What do you think he's like? With a partner, ask and answer the questions in **A** about him.

C 🔊 **Listen for details.** Silvia and her friend are on her computer. Listen. Circle the best answers. **CD 1 Track 3**

1. His name is _Lars_ .
   a. Lawrence   b. Lars   c. Larry
2. He speaks _four_ languages.
   a. two   b. three   c. four
3. He's from _Sweden_ .
   a. Switzerland   b. England   c. Sweden
4. His hometown is _Visby_ .
   a. Stockholm   b. Visby   c. Bern
5. He's a _busines_ student.
   a. business   b. math   c. science
6. He's interested in travel and _music_ .
   a. music   b. languages   c. movies

D ⟳ In your notebook, complete the sentences in **C** about your best friend. Change pronouns if needed. Tell a partner about your friend.

E ⟳ What are you interested in? Check the boxes. Then ask a partner about his or her answers.

I'm interested in…

- ☐ music.
- ☑ languages.
- ☑ travel.
- ☐ video games.
- ☑ sports.
- ☐ cooking.
- ☐ movies.
- ☐ your idea: _____

> I like music and video games.

> Really? I'm interested in music, too. What's your favorite kind of music?

4 SPEAKING

A 🔊 Mariana and Danny live in the same apartment building. Listen. Are they meeting for the first time? How do you know? **CD 1 Track 4**

MARIANA: Hi. My name is Mariana. I'm in apartment 201.

DANNY: Hi, Mariana. I'm Danny. I'm in 302. It's nice to meet you.

MARIANA: Nice to meet you, too.

DANNY: So, are you a student, Mariana?

MARIANA: Yeah, I study music at NYU.

DANNY: That's interesting.

MARIANA: What do you do, Danny?

DANNY: I'm a student at Hunter College. I also work in an art gallery.

B 🔄 Practice the conversation with a partner. Then practice with *your* information.

SPEAKING STRATEGY

C 👥 Introduce yourself to four classmates. Then ask about their names and occupations. Complete the chart with their information. Use the Useful Expressions to help you.

Useful Expressions	
Introducing yourself	**Asking about occupations**
A: My name is Mariana.	A: What do you do?
B: Hi, I'm Danny. (It's) Nice to meet you.	B: I'm a music student.
A: (It's) Nice to meet you, too.	
Speaking tip	
When you are introducing yourself, *My name is*... and *I'm*... can both be used.	

Name	Occupation
Clara	student (studies art)
1. My name is Mariana	I am a music student
2. My name is Danny	I am a student at Hunter College. I also working in an art gallery
3.	
4.	

D 🔄 Tell a partner about the classmates you talked to in **C**.

> Clara is a student. She studies art.

5 GRAMMAR

A Turn to page 195. Complete the exercise. Then do **B–E** below.

Review of the Simple Present Tense		
	Questions	**Answers**
Yes / No questions with be	**Are** you a student?	Yes, I **am**. / No, I**'m** not.
	Is he a student?	Yes, he **is**. / No, he**'s** not.
Yes / No questions with other verbs	**Do** you **speak** English?	Yes, I **do**. / No, I **don't**.
	Does she **speak** English?	Yes, she **does**. / No, she **doesn't**.
Wh- questions	What do you do?	I'm a student.
	What does she do?	She's a doctor.

B Steffi is writing about herself and her classmate. Read the sentences. Write the correct form of each verb.

Monika and Me

Monika (1. be) ___is___ my classmate. We (2. be) _haVe_ different in many ways. I (3. be) ___am___ an only child. Monika (4. have) ___a___ two brothers and a sister. I (5. live) _in Sacramento_ with my family. Monika (6. live) _in Sacr_ in her own apartment. We both go to Western University, but I (7. study) _E S L_ English literature and Monika (8. study) _____ business. I (9. not have) _____ a job, but Monika (10. work) _____ part-time in a cafe. I (11. love) _____ dance music, but Monika (12. not like) _____ it. She (13. listen) _____ to rap. Monika and I (14. watch) _____ TV together on the weekends.

C Complete questions 1–4 with the correct form of *be* or *do*. Complete questions 5–8 with a *Wh-* question word. Take turns asking and answering the questions with a partner.

1. _____ Steffi and Monika different?
2. _____ Steffi an only child?
3. _____ Steffi study business?
4. _____ Monika and Steffi go to the same university?

5. _____ subject does Steffi study?
6. _____ does Monika work?
7. _____ does Steffi live with?
8. _____ does Monika live?

D Complete each sentence with an affirmative or negative verb in the box to make it true for you.

speak	have	study	like

1. I _____ a middle name.
2. I _____ my first name.
3. I _Speak_ more than one language well.

4. I _____ on the weekend.
5. I _____ my hometown.
6. I _____ a favorite subject at school.

E How are you and your partner similar and different? Use the sentences in **D** to form questions. Ask follow-up questions.

Do you have a middle name? → Yes, I do. → What is it? → It's Victor.

6 COMMUNICATION

A 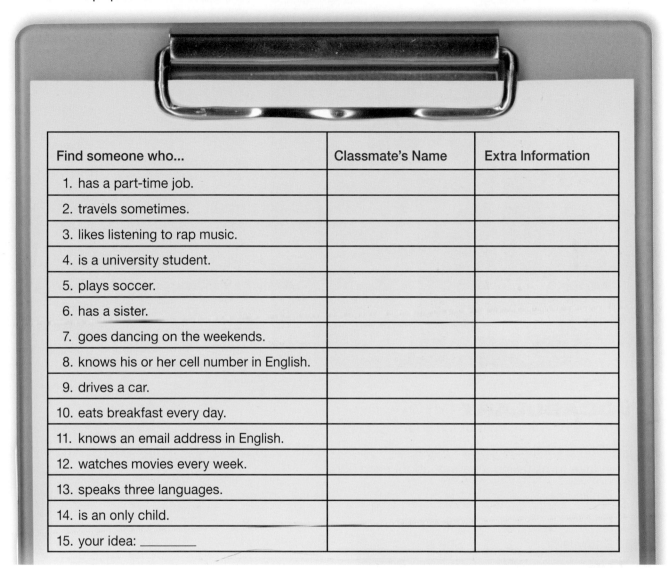 For each item in the chart, ask the question until you find a person who answers *Yes*. Write his or her name. Then ask one follow-up question and write the extra information.

> **i** Follow-up questions are an important part of conversation. Make sure to ask a follow-up question related to what your partner already said. *Wh-* questions usually work better than *Yes / No* questions.

Find someone who...	Classmate's Name	Extra Information
1. has a part-time job.		
2. travels sometimes.		
3. likes listening to rap music.		
4. is a university student.		
5. plays soccer.		
6. has a sister.		
7. goes dancing on the weekends.		
8. knows his or her cell number in English.		
9. drives a car.		
10. eats breakfast every day.		
11. knows an email address in English.		
12. watches movies every week.		
13. speaks three languages.		
14. is an only child.		
15. your idea: _____		

Do you have a part-time job?

Yes, I do.

What do you do?

I work in a bookstore.

B Tell a classmate about the people in your chart.

Michael, 19

Emilio, 52

Alexis, 23   Ashley, 23

Kathy, 48

Use *be* with...	Use *have* with...
Age	**Eye color**
young	(dark) brown
in his / her teens*	blue
in his / her twenties*	green
elderly (80+)	
	Hairstyle
Weight	long ↔ short
skinny	straight ↔ curly
thin	wavy
slim**	spiky
average weight	
heavy	**Hair color**
	black
Height	(light / dark) brown
short	blond
average height	red
tall	gray
	Facial hair
	beard
	mustache

*teens (13–19), twenties (ages 20–29), thirties, forties

**Slim means skinny / thin, but slim has a positive meaning.

1 VOCABULARY

A 🔁 Complete the sentences about each person in the family photo. Use the words in the box. Then take turns telling a partner about each person.

1. Emilio is ____in his fifties____. He is ____tall____. He is ____average weight____.

    age   height   weight

He has ____brown____ eyes. He has ____short____, ____gray____ hair.

2. Kathy is ____48____. She is _____. She is _____.

    age   height   weight

She has _____ eyes. She has _____, straight, _____ hair.

3. Michael is _____. He is _____. He is _____.

    age   height   weight

He has _____ eyes. He has _____, _____, _____ hair.

4. Alexis and Ashley are _____. They are _____. They are _____.

               age   height   weight

They have _____ eyes. They have _____, wavy hair.

B 🔁 Answer the questions with a partner.

1. Who does Michael look like?   He **looks like** ____his father____. They're both tall.

2. Who does Ashley look like?   She **looks like** _____. They both have red hair.

3. Who do you look like?   I **look like** _____. We're both... / We both have...

> I look like my mom. We're both tall and slim, and we both have dark, curly hair.

2 LISTENING

A 🔄 **Use background knowledge.** Look at the pictures below. Describe the man's appearance in each one. Tell a partner.

a. ☐

b. ☐

c. ☐

B 🔊 **Listen for gist.** Read the sentence below. Then listen and complete it.

Emily is at the airport. She is ____ her uncle Tim. **CD 1 Track 5**

a. traveling with   b. looking for   c. talking to   d. shopping for

C 🔊 **Listen for details.** Now listen to the entire conversation. Circle the words that describe Uncle Tim before and now. Then check (✓) the correct picture of Uncle Tim <u>now</u> in **A**. **CD 1 Track 6**

1. Uncle Tim <u>before</u>:

    short / **tall**   short hair / **long hair**   **brown hair** / blond hair

2. Uncle Tim <u>now</u>:

    short / **tall**   **short hair** / long hair   brown hair / **blond hair**

D 🔄 Think about your appearance in the past. Is anything different now? Complete the sentences. Tell a partner.

In the past, I was _short, and I had short black hair._

Now I am _taller and my hair is so long._

In the past, I had _highligts in my hair._

Now I have _just black hair._

> In the past, I had short, brown hair. Now I have long, blond hair.

3 READING

A 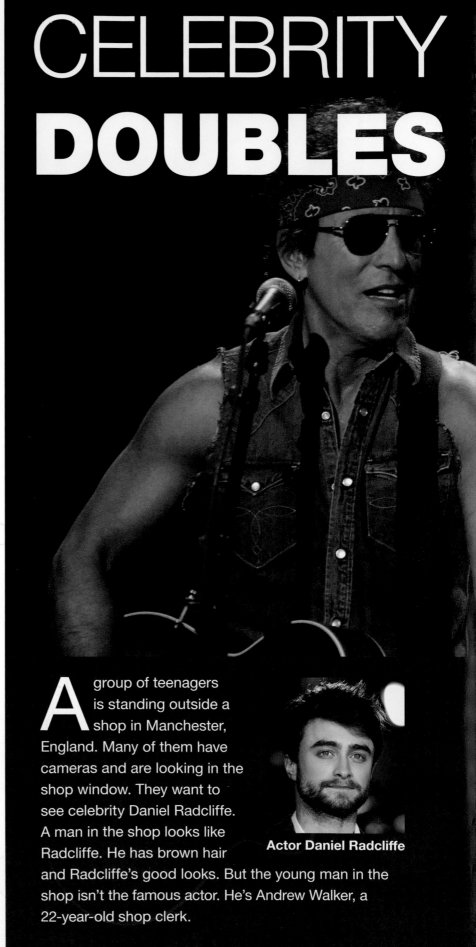 Look at the photo. Who are these people? What do they do? Tell a partner.

B **Skim for gist.** Read the passage. Then complete the sentence below.

The reading is mainly about _____.

a. the actor Daniel Radcliffe

b. people who look like celebrities

c. good-looking actors

d. famous people with a lot of money

C **Scan for details.** Quickly find and underline the answers to questions 1 and 2 in the reading.

1. How does Andrew Walker make money?

2. How do celebrity doubles make money?

D 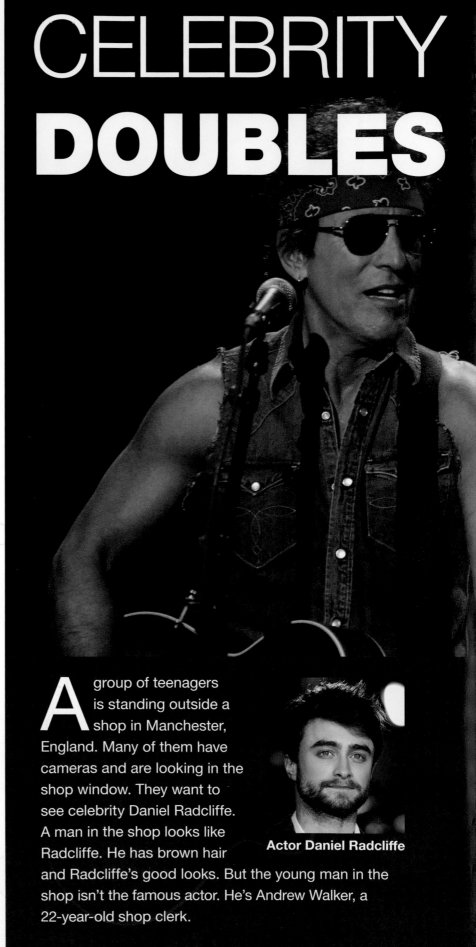 Answer the questions with a partner.

1. Look at the photo of the two men singing. Do they look alike? Why or why not?

2. Is being a celebrity double fun? Why or why not?

3. Do you (or someone you know) look like a famous person? Who? Explain.

CELEBRITY DOUBLES

Actor Daniel Radcliffe

A group of teenagers is standing outside a shop in Manchester, England. Many of them have cameras and are looking in the shop window. They want to see celebrity Daniel Radcliffe. A man in the shop looks like Radcliffe. He has brown hair and Radcliffe's good looks. But the young man in the shop isn't the famous actor. He's Andrew Walker, a 22-year-old shop clerk.

Comedian Jimmy Fallon (right) and musician Bruce Springsteen perform together.

Walker isn't surprised by the teenagers. People often stop him on the street and want to take his picture. Walker is a clerk, but he also makes money as Radcliffe's double. Walker travels all over Europe as Daniel Radcliffe. It's an exciting life for the shop clerk from Manchester.

Today, many companies work with celebrity doubles. The most popular celebrity doubles look like famous athletes, pop singers, and actors. The companies pay doubles to go to parties and business meetings. Doubles are also on TV and in commercials.

Some celebrities even dress up as doubles. American talk show host Jimmy Fallon is famous for dressing up and performing as famous musicians. He looks and sounds just like them. Sometimes the real musicians even come on his show!

4 GRAMMAR

A Turn to page 196. Complete the exercises. Then do **B–D** below.

Describing Appearance			
Subject	***be / have***	**Adjective**	**Noun**
He	is	tall.	
		average	height / weight.
		young / in his teens.	
	has	blue	eyes.
		spiky, black	hair.

B 🔄 Work with a partner. Practice the conversation. Can you guess the person? Check your answer on the bottom of the page.

A: I'm thinking of a famous person.

B: Is it a woman?

A: No, it's a man.

B: Is he British?

A: No, he's not. He's from Argentina.

B: Is he tall?

A: No, he's not. He's a little short.

B: Is he in his twenties?

A: Yes, I think he's in his late twenties.

B: Does he have long hair?

A: No, he doesn't.

B: Is he a soccer player?

A: Yes, he is.

B: I know! It's…

C Think of a famous person. Complete the notes below.

Name: _____   Hair: _____   Height: _____

Job: _____   Eyes: _____   Weight: _____

Nationality: _____   Age: _____

D 🔄 Ask your partner seven questions. Try to guess his or her person. Then switch roles.

5 WRITING

A Read the paragraph on the right. Then write five or six sentences about a classmate's appearance on a separate piece of paper. Use the paragraph as a model. Don't write your classmate's name.

> My classmate is in his twenties. He's average height—he's about 172 centimeters. He has short, straight, brown hair. He has dark brown eyes (I think). He doesn't wear glasses.

B 🔄 Exchange papers with a partner.

1. Are there any mistakes in your partner's writing? If yes, circle them.

2. Can you guess the person? Write his or her name on the paper.

Answer B: Lionel Messi!

6 COMMUNICATION

A 👥 Work in a group of four. Each person chooses a photo above. Think about your answers to the questions below.

1. What does the person in your photo look like? Describe him or her.

2. In your opinion, is the person good-looking? Why or why not?

B 👥 Tell the group your answers in **A**. Do your partners agree with you? Why or why not?

> I think he's very handsome.

> He's OK. I don't like his beard or hairstyle.

Word Bank
Other words to describe appearance
Has...
a nice smile
a tattoo
Is...
pretty
handsome
good-looking

C 👥 Now find a photo of someone else online. Show it to your group. Then repeat **A** and **B**.

2 BEHAVIOR

Look at the photo. Answer the questions.

1 What are these people doing?

2 How do they feel?

3 Why do you think they feel that way?

UNIT GOALS

1 Talk about actions happening now

2 Greet other people and ask how they are

3 Describe how you feel

4 Talk about and use common gestures

A tango performance in Buenos Aires, Argentina

1 VIDEO Can You Spot a Fake Smile?

Word Bank

fake = not real

genuine = real

to spot = to see; to notice

to smile = to raise the corners
of your mouth

A Look at this photo. Are the smiles genuine or not? Why do you think so? Tell a partner.

B Watch the video. You are going to see three pairs of photos. Choose the person with the <u>fake</u> smile in each pair.

1. LEFT   RIGHT
2. LEFT   RIGHT
3. LEFT   RIGHT

Scoring

3 correct answers: You're good at spotting a fake smile.

2 correct answers: You're OK.

0–1 correct answers: You can't spot a fake smile.

C Could you spot the fake smiles? Compare your score with a partner's score.

D Watch again. Circle the correct answer. Do you agree with the answer?

To spot a fake smile, look at the person's eyes / face / mouth.

2 VOCABULARY

A Work with a partner. Read these sentences. Who is doing what? Match the sentences to the people in the picture. Write the correct letter. Not all letters will be used.

1. She's **smiling** at her friend. _b_
2. She's **pointing** at the man. _f_
3. He's **shouting** at the woman. _e_
4. She's **waving** goodbye to her daughter. _d_
5. She's **talking** to her friend. _a_

6. It's **barking** at the girl. _h_
7. He's **looking** outside. _c_
8. She's **sitting** on the bench. _g_
9. She's **walking** down the street. _j_
10. She's **running**. _i_

B Now cover up the sentences in **A**. Work with a partner. Take turns describing the picture. Try to talk about all of the people.

> Let's see... two women are talking and walking together. I think they are friends....

3 LISTENING

A 🔊 **Pronunciation: Listening for contractions.** Read the sentences. Then listen and repeat. Notice the difference between the sentences in each pair. **CD 1 Track 8**

(1a.) I am talking to you!   (3a.) We are too busy today.

1b. I'm talking to you!   3b. We're too busy today.

2a. Oh yes, it is mine. Thanks!   4a. How is it going?

(2b.) Oh yes, it's mine. Thanks!   (4b.) How's it going?

B 🔊 **Pronunciation: Listening for contractions.** Now listen to four short dialogs. For each one, circle the sentence in **A** that you hear. **CD 1 Track 9**

C 🔊 **Distinguish speakers.** Look at the picture on page 19 as you listen to these five conversations. Write the letters of the people from the picture speaking in each one. **CD 1 Track 10**

Conversation 1: _d_   Conversation 4: _i_ _j_

Conversation 2: _f_ _l_   Conversation 5: _b_ _a_

Conversation 3: _c_ _k_

D 🔊 **Infer information.** Listen again. Match each situation with the appropriate verb. One verb is extra. **CD 1 Track 10**

asking	looking	saying
helping	meeting	shouting

1. The woman is _saying_ goodbye to her daughter.

2. The woman is _helping_ the man.

3. The man is _shouting_ at the woman.

4. The girl is _asking_ her mother something.

5. The two friends are _meeting_

E 🔊 👥 Listen to Conversation 5 again. With a partner, write an ending to it. Then role-play your conversation for another pair. **CD 1 Track 11**

4 SPEAKING

A 🔊 🔁 Read the conversation and listen. Why is Katy worried? What is Jim's idea? Tell a partner. **CD 1 Track 12**

JIM: Hi, Katy.

KATY: Hey, Jim. How's it going?

JIM: Great! How are you doing?

KATY: So-so.

JIM: Yeah? What's wrong?

KATY: Oh, I have an important test tomorrow.

JIM: But you're not studying.

KATY: Well, I'm kind of tired.

JIM: Why don't you take a break and drink some coffee? We can go to a cafe together.

KATY: And then I can study later. Sounds good!

B 🔁 Practice the conversation with a partner. Then ask your partner how he or she is today.

SPEAKING STRATEGY

C 🔁 Read the two situations below. With a partner, write two new conversations on a sheet of paper. Use the conversation in **A** and the Useful Expressions to help you.

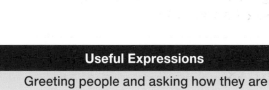

Useful Expressions
Greeting people and asking how they are
☺ A: Hi, _Katy_. How's it going?
B: Fine. / OK. / All right. / Pretty good. / Not bad. How about you?
A: I'm fine.
☹ A: Hi, _Jim_. How are you doing?
B: So-so. / Not so good.
A: Really? What's wrong?
B: I'm (a little) worried. / I'm (kind of) tired. I have a big test tomorrow.

Situation 1

Student A: You're worried. You have two tickets to a basketball game tonight. You're going with your friend, but your friend is late.

Student B: Your suggestion: Take a taxi to the game. Maybe the friend is there.

Situation 2

Student A: You're unhappy. You live in Toronto. Your cousin lives in Boston. She wants you to visit her. Plane tickets are expensive right now.

Student B: Your suggestion: Rent a car and drive from Toronto to Boston.

Word Bank
kind of = a little

D 👥 Role-play one conversation for another pair.

5 GRAMMAR

A Turn to page 197. Complete the exercise. Then do **B** and **C** below.

Review of the Present Continuous Tense			
Affirmative and negative statements			
I'm / She's / They're	(not)	going	to the party.

Wh- and Yes / No questions					**Answers**
	Are	you	going	to the party?	Yes, I am. / No, I'm not.
When	are				In about an hour.

Use the present continuous for actions happening now: subject + *am* / *is* / *are* + verb *-ing*

B Ask and answer questions about the people in the picture.

1a. Where are they ___sitting___? On the sofa.

1b. What are they ___drinking___? Coffee.

2. ___Are___ they talking? No, they're ___not___.

3. ___Is___ she opening a present? Yes, she ___is___.

4. ___Is___ he enjoying the music? No, he ___isn't___.

C 🔄 Take turns acting out one of the actions below for your partner. You can also add your own ideas to the list.

driving a car / riding a bicycle / riding a horse

waking up late / taking a shower / brushing your teeth

eating noodles / eating an ice cream cone / eating steak

drinking coffee / drinking juice / drinking soda

putting on a pair of jeans / putting on a winter coat / putting on a pair of boots

your own ideas: _____

> Let's see... you're drinking something. I know, it's juice! No? OK then, maybe you're drinking...

6 COMMUNICATION

A Think of a place in your city or a famous place in the world. Write it down. (Don't show anyone!)

_____

B Imagine you are in the place you wrote down in **A**.
What do you see? What are people doing?
Write four or five sentences about your place.
See the example for ideas.

Example: It's a beautiful city. There is a lot of water. Some people are riding in a boat. A man is standing in the boat. He is pushing. They are going under a bridge.

Venice, Italy

_____
_____
_____
_____
_____

C 🔄 Do the following:

Student A: Read your sentences from **B** to a partner.

Student B: Draw the place your partner describes in the box below.

Student A: Check your partner's drawing. Is it accurate? Can your partner guess the place?

D 🔄 Switch roles and do **C** again.

confident

relaxed

| embarrassed | ~~relaxed~~ | excited | bored | confused |
| nervous / worried | sad | happy | angry | ~~confident~~ |

1 VOCABULARY

A Look at the photos. How do the people feel? Point to a photo and tell a partner. Then write the correct word under each photo.

> She's angry.

B Work with a partner.

1. **Student A:** Choose one feeling and act it out for your partner.
   Student B: Close your book. Guess your partner's feeling.
2. Change roles and repeat step 1. Do this until you act out all the feelings.

C Ask and answer the questions below with a partner. Use a word from **A**. Explain your answers.

How do you feel...

- when you're waiting for the bus?
- before a big exam?
- when you speak English?

- about summer vacation?
- when a friend is always late?
- right now?

> **i** Say *I feel* <u>bored</u>.
> NOT ~~I feel boring~~.

2 LISTENING

A 🔊 **Understand a speaker's attitude.** Read sentences 1a–4a. Then listen. Circle the correct answer. **CD 1 Track 13**

How do they feel?	Why?
1a. The man is excited about / bored with school.	1b. He wants to ___*Shens*___ his major.
2a. The woman is worried / confident about her exams.	2b. She ___*know*___ the information.
3a. The man is confident / confused about the address of the theater.	3b. The map on his phone is ___*mg*___.
4a. The woman's boss is worried / angry. The woman is embarrassed / excited.	4b. The woman is *embarras* for work.

B 🔊 **Listen for details.** Listen again. Complete sentences 1b–4b with one word. **CD 1 Track 13**

C 🔄 Look at the gestures. Complete each sentence with an expression from the box. Check your answers with a partner.

Come here	Good luck	I don't know	Look (at that)

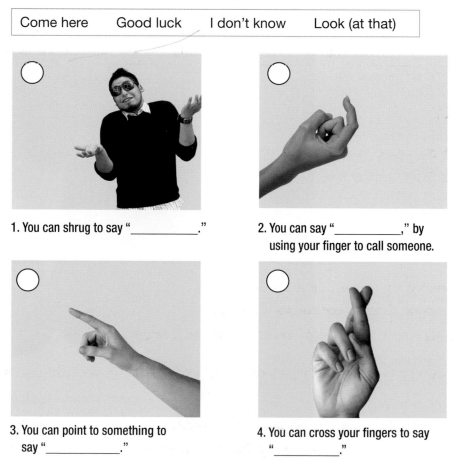

1. You can shrug to say "_____."

2. You can say "_____," by using your finger to call someone.

3. You can point to something to say "_____."

4. You can cross your fingers to say "_____."

D 🔊 **Infer information.** Listen again. Which gesture in **C** could be used in each conversation? Write the number of the conversation (1–4) on each photo. **CD 1 Track 13**

E 🔄 Do the gestures in the photos have the same meaning in your country? Tell a partner.

3 READING

WORLD GREETINGS

press noses together

A Preview the reading. Look at the title and photos. Complete the definition and answer the question with a partner.

A *greeting* is a way to say _____.

What are the people in the photos doing?

B Make predictions; Scan for details. Guess where people use the greetings below: Brazil, New Zealand, or Japan? Write the country or countries. Then scan the reading to check your ideas.

Greeting	Country
1. bow	_____
2. kiss	_____
3. press noses	_____
4. shake hands	_____
5. wave	_____

C Read for details. These sentences are false. Read the article. Make them true. Tell a partner.

1. In Brazil, women kiss other women as a greeting. Women don't kiss men.

2. When you shake hands, don't look at the person.

3. The Maori are the native people of Brazil.

4. In Japan, a smile always means you are happy.

D In each situation below, what greeting do you use? What do you say? Tell a partner.

1. You see a friend in a cafe.

2. You interview for a job with Mr. Jones.

3. You meet your teacher on the street.

4. You see your boyfriend or girlfriend.

WORLD LINK

Go online and learn about another country. Answer these questions:

1. How do friends greet each other? Is it the same for men and women? How about between an older person and a younger one?

2. In the workplace, how do people greet each other?

Brazil

Men often shake hands when they meet for the first time. When women meet, they touch cheeks and kiss. Women also kiss male friends to say hello.

Note: When you shake hands, look at the person. It's polite.[1]

kiss

New Zealand

In formal situations, both men and women usually shake hands when they meet someone for the first time. In informal situations, people often give a short wave and say "Hi."

Note: If you see two people pressing their noses together, they are probably Maori. The Maori are the native people of New Zealand. This is their traditional greeting.

shake hands

Japan

When people meet for the first time, they usually bow. In business, people also shake hands. In formal situations, people often exchange business cards. When you give a business card, it's polite to give it with two hands.

Note: In Japan, a smile can have different meanings. It usually means that the person is happy or that the person thinks something is funny. But it can also mean that the person is embarrassed.

bow

[1]If you are *polite*, you act in a respectful way.

4 GRAMMAR

A Turn to page 198. Complete the exercises. Then do **B–D** below.

ℹ️ **Object pronouns** come after...
a verb: My parents *love* **me**.
a preposition: Jon is angry *at* **her**.

Subject Pronouns	Object Pronouns
<u>I</u> love my parents.	My parents love **me**.
<u>You</u> need help.	I can help **you**.*
<u>He</u> / <u>She</u> knows Jon.	Jon knows **him** / **her**.
<u>It</u> is expensive.	I can't buy **it**.
<u>We</u> are having a party.	Please join **us**.
<u>They</u> are popular.	Everyone likes **them**.

*For both singular and plural *you*

B Complete the sentences with the correct object pronoun(s).

1. I speak English at school. Sometimes, I use _____ at home, too.

2. I have to take the university entrance exam soon. I'm worried about _____.

3. My cell phone is cool. My parents gave _____ to _____.

4. When I watch movies in English, I get confused. People talk fast. I can't understand _____.

5. Do you understand this grammar point? I can explain _____ to _____.

6. We are studying English. It can help _____ get jobs in the future.

7. _____ is my best friend. I talk to _____ every day.

C 🔁 Work with a partner. Check your answers in **B**. Which sentences are true for you? Which aren't? Why?

D 🔁 Which sentences in **B** aren't true for you? Change them so they are true and tell them to your partner.

5 WRITING

A 🔁 Koji and Paloma are classmates. They're texting. Match the underlined expressions with their meanings below. Then tell a partner: How does Paloma feel?

1. Are you _____

2. face-to-face _____

3. How are you? _____

4. OK _____

5. See you later. _____

6. Thanks. _____

B 🔁 With your partner, complete the rules for texting. Can you think of other rules?

In texts, it's OK…	In informal situations (with friends)	In formal situations (with a teacher or boss)
1. not to capitalize words.	☑	☐
2. not to use punctuation.	☐	☐
3. to use abbreviations.	☐	☐
4. to use emoticons (smiley faces).	☐	☐

C 🔁 In your notebook, rewrite the text conversation in **A** in full sentences. Add any missing words. Use correct punctuation and capitalization. Compare answers with a partner.

D 🔁 Write a text to a partner in English. Use the expressions and emoticons in **A**. Do the following:

Student A: Imagine you have a school project to do. How do you feel? Text your partner.

Student B: Reply to your partner's text. Suggest working on the project together.

Student A: Agree and suggest a time to meet.

Student B: Reply to your partner's text.

Student A: Say "bye."

Student B: Say "bye."

E 🔁 Read your partner's text and correct any mistakes. Then write a short reply to your partner to reschedule the meeting time.

6 COMMUNICATION

A 👥 Get into a group of three people. Read the directions to play this game.

Student A: Choose a sentence below. Act out the sentence for Students B and C. Do *not* use words.

Students B and C: Watch Student A. Be the first to say the sentence Student A is acting out. If you guess correctly, you get a point.

Take turns acting out the sentences. Play until all sentences are done.

I'm hungry.	Good luck!	He's crazy.
This is delicious.	Go away!	I'm nervous.
Stop it!	Look at that!	This tastes terrible.
Let's go!	Come here!	I'm not listening!
Be quiet.	I'm bored.	Sit down.
I'm sad.	I'm angry.	See you later.
Relax!	What? I can't hear you.	I'm not sure.

I know! You're saying "Come here!"

3 SHOPPING

BALLY

Look at the photo. Answer the questions.

1 Is there a shopping mall in your city? What is it called?

2 Do you ever go to these kinds of stores?
- a department store
- a coffee shop
- a clothing store
- a supermarket

3 What are the stores' names? What do you buy there?

UNIT GOALS

1 Identify common foods

2 Talk about things you need

3 Describe your shopping habits

4 Discuss different places to shop and what they sell

A luxury shopping mall in Berlin, Germany

Farmers' markets are growing around the world. This one is in Otavalo, Ecuador.

1 **VIDEO** Field of Greens

A Look at the photo. What do you see? Do you have any markets like this in your city?

B ▶ 🔁 Watch the video. What fruits and vegetables do you see? Make a list in your notebook. Compare your list to a partner's.

C ▶ Watch the video again. Then answer the questions.

1. What is unusual about the first farm in the video?

2. Do farmers' markets sell foods besides *produce* (fruits and vegetables)?

3. What are the main benefits of shopping at farmers' markets?

D 🔁 With a partner, plan a dinner menu. Use foods that you can find at a farmers' market. Share your menu with the class. Which pair has the best menu?

2 VOCABULARY

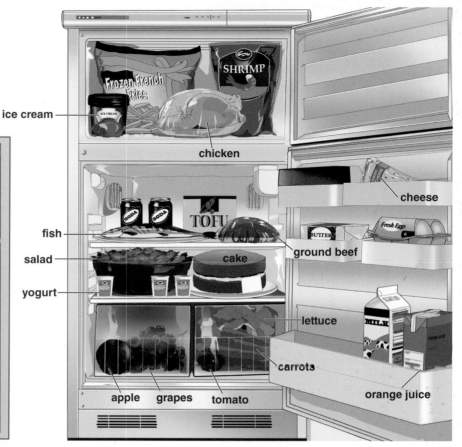

A 🗣️ Practice saying the items in the picture with a partner. Which of these foods do you eat? Tell your partner.

B 🗣️ Work with your partner. On a piece of paper, copy the chart below. Think of examples for each type of food. Use words from the picture and your own ideas.

Fresh foods	Frozen foods	Junk foods	Breakfast foods	Foods you eat every day

C 👥 Share your chart with another pair. Then ask and answer these questions.

1. What is one thing in your chart that isn't in the picture above?

2. Which items in your chart do you like? Are there any items you *don't* like to eat or drink?

3 LISTENING

A 🔊 **Pronunciation: Syllables.** Practice saying the words aloud. Then listen and repeat. **CD 1 Track 15**

1. fish   2. soda   3. potato

B 🔊 👥 **Pronunciation: Syllables.** Work with a partner. Read each word aloud. How many syllables does it have: one, two, or three? Guess. Then listen and check your answers. **CD 1 Track 16**

		1	2	3			1	2	3
1.	milk	☑	☐	☐	6.	cake	☑	☐	☐
2.	carrots	☐	☑	☐	7.	yogurt	☐	☑	☐
3.	tomato	☐	☐	☑	8.	apple	☐	☑	☐
4.	cheese	☑	☐	☐	9.	cereal	☐	☐	☑
5.	banana	☐	☐	☑					

C 👥 **Use background knowledge.** Look at the two pictures below. What's in each bag? Make two lists. Tell a partner.

D 🔊 **Listen for gist.** Listen. Which shopping bag is Allison's? Circle it. **CD 1 Track 17**

ice cream

E 🔊 **Listen for details.** Listen. Allison's mom changes one item on the list. Put an *X* on the item in the shopping bag. Write the name of the new item. **CD 1 Track 18**

_____

F 🔊 **Listen for details.** How do Allison and her mom talk about the foods they need? Match the items on the left with the words on the right. Then listen and check your answers. **CD 1 Track 19**

1. I need a _loaf_ of bread.   a. bunch
2. And a _head_ of lettuce.   b. head
3. A _carton_ of ice cream.   c. carton
4. Please get a _bunch_ of carrots, OK?   d. loaf

G 👥 Cover your answers in **D–F** and tell a partner: What items does Allison buy for her mom?

4 SPEAKING

A 🔊 Read the conversation and listen. Underline the foods Ken and Rachel have. Circle the foods they need. **CD 1 Track 20**

KEN: Rachel, I'm making a shopping list for our barbecue. We have **chicken**. What else do we need?

RACHEL: Let's see... we need some **potatoes**.

KEN: Okay, got it.

RACHEL: We also need **lettuce** and **tomatoes** for the salad.

KEN: And what about drinks?

RACHEL: Let's see... we have **soda**.

KEN: Okay. I'll buy some **juice** then. See you!

B 🔁 Practice the conversation with a partner. Then make your own conversation. Use your own ideas for the **bold** words.

SPEAKING STRATEGY

C Imagine you are having a class party. Everyone in the class must bring something to the party. Think of an idea and write it on the board.

D 🔁 Work with a partner. Look at the checklist below. These are things you need for the party. Look at the items on the board. Use the Useful Expressions to talk about the things you have and the things you need for your party.

<u>Class Party Checklist</u>

food

drinks

dessert

napkins, cups, plates

forks, spoons, knives, chopsticks

chairs

Useful Expressions
Talking about things you need
Do we need anything?
Yes, we do. We need soda and bottled water.
Let's see... we need...
No, we don't. We (already) have everything.
What else do we need?
We still need...
Nothing. I think we're all set.
Anything else?
Yes, we need...
No, that's it. We have everything.
Speaking tip
You can use *let's see* when you are thinking carefully about something.

E 👥 Share your ideas in **D** with another pair.

5 GRAMMAR

A Turn to page 199. Complete the exercise. Then do **B**–**F** below.

Count and Noncount Nouns	
Count	**Noncount**
a tomato, an apple	bread, rice
two carrots, three eggs	coffee, sugar

B Study the chart above. With a partner, write *C* or *N* to say if each phrase describes count or noncount nouns.

1. _____ can follow *a* or *an*

2. _____ can follow numbers

3. _____ are always singular

4. _____ have singular and plural forms

C Complete the sentences with *a* or *an*. If no article is needed, leave the space blank.

1. Do you want _____ rice or _____ baked potato with your dinner?

2. Billy wants _____ fruit. Give him _____ apple.

3. Do you usually put _____ sugar in _____ tea?

4. I often eat _____ banana as a snack.

5. Is there _____ salt in this soup?

6. I have _____ cereal and _____ egg every morning for breakfast.

D Read the sentences. Circle *T* for true or *F* for false. Use your own information.

1. I don't like soda because it has too much sugar.   Ⓣ   F

2. I usually eat pasta once or twice a week.   T   Ⓕ

3. You can usually find apples, oranges, or some kind of fruit in my refrigerator.   Ⓣ   F

4. I eat more bread than rice.   T   Ⓕ

5. I drink at least two glasses of water a day.   T   Ⓕ

6. I need coffee in the morning to wake up.   T   Ⓕ

7. I don't eat hot soup in the summer.   T   Ⓕ

8. I eat too much cake.   Ⓣ   F

E Which nouns in **D** are count? Which are noncount? Tell a partner.

F Compare your answers in **D** with your partner's.

> Soda has too much sugar, but I like it.

> Me too. I drink a can of soda every day.

6 COMMUNICATION

A Read about this TV show. Think about what it would be like to live on the island.

There is a new reality show on TV. On this show, people stay on an island in the Pacific Ocean for one month to win money. Here is some information about the island:

- There are a lot of fish in the ocean.
- On the island, there are a lot of coconuts and fruit trees. There's also a lot of sand!
- There's very little water to drink on the island.
- In the afternoon, it is very hot (100 degrees F / 38 degrees C).

B You want to be on the show. For your stay on the island, you can choose six items from the list below. Is there anything you want to add to the list? Write it. Then circle the six items you need.

meat	toothpaste	bananas	bandages	a knife
bottled water	soap	oranges	coffee or tea	matches
rice	sunscreen	magazines	toilet paper	_bottled water_
bread	a hat	shampoo	vitamins	_vitamins_

C 👥 Join a group of three or four people. Compare your answers. Explain your choices. Together make *one* list of six items.

> There's very little water on the island. We need to bring water.

D 👥 Explain your final list to the class.

1 VOCABULARY

Word Bank

go shopping = shop (for something)

Opposites

affordable ↔ **expensive**

buy ↔ **sell**

credit or **debit card** ↔ **cash**

on sale ↔ **full price**

A   Read the sentences. Review the meaning of the words in **blue** with your instructor. Then complete the sentences so they are true for you.

1. I usually **shop** for things _____.

   a. alone   b. with one person   c. with a group

2. I **buy** most of my clothes _____.

   a. online   b. at stores in **a mall**   c. in my neighborhood

3. I _____ buy things **on sale**. The price is lower, so the items are more **affordable**.

   a. often   b. sometimes   c. never

4. I **spend** _____ **money** on electronics (computers, phones) each year.

   a. a lot of   b. some   c. no

5. I **pay** for most things with _____.

   a. **cash**   b. a **debit card**   c. a **credit card**

B   Tell a partner your answers in **A**. Your partner asks you one follow-up question.

> I buy most of my clothes at stores in a mall.

> What's your favorite store?

2 LISTENING

A Look at the photos above and the list of stores below. Write the correct number (1–4) on each picture. Then write the correct letter (a–d) on each line to match the items with the stores.

Stores

1. a candy store _c_
2. an electronics store _a_
3. a jewelry store _d_
4. a thrift store _b_

Items

a. computers, phones
b. used clothes and furniture
c. chocolate
d. rings, necklaces

B 🔊 **Listen for gist.** Listen. In each conversation, the people are shopping. Where are they? Write *1*, *2*, or *3*. One store is extra. **CD 1 Track 21**

_3_ a candy store   _1_ an electronics store   ____ a jewelry store   _2_ a thrift store

C 🔊 **Listen for details.** Read the sentences. Then listen again. Circle the correct answer. **CD 1 Track 21**

Store 1

1. The man is shopping for ____.
   a. candy   b. a ring   (c.) a phone
2. The man ____.
   (a.) goes to another store
   b. spends a lot of money
   c. buys something affordable

Store 2

1. The ____ like(s) the store a lot.
   a. man   (b.) woman   c. man and woman
2. The woman says the coat is ____.
   a. expensive   (b.) affordable   c. on sale

Store 3

1. The items in this store are ____.
   (a.) expensive   b. affordable   c. on sale
2. The man pays with ____.
   a. cash   (b.) a credit card   c. a debit card

D 🔄 Do you ever shop at any of the places in **A**? If yes, what do you buy? Tell a partner.

3 READING

A 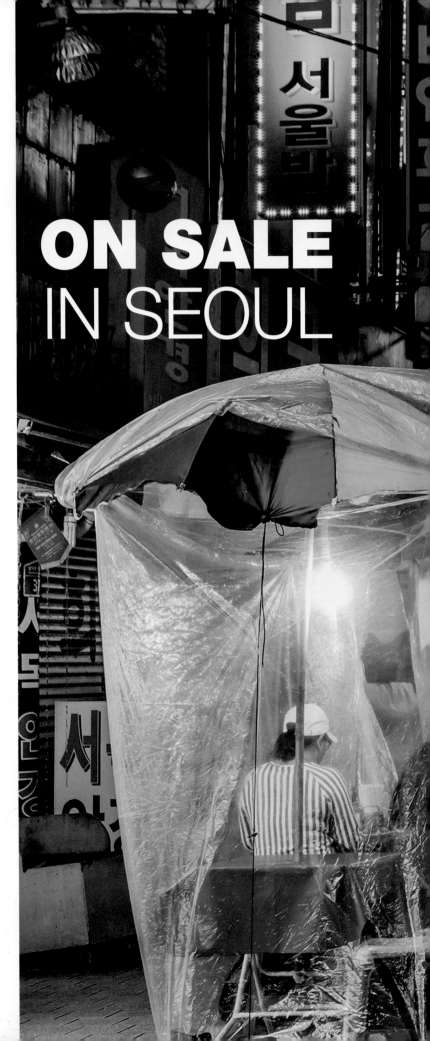 **Make predictions.** Read the title. Is the article about expensive or affordable stores in Seoul? Tell a partner.

B **Identify main ideas.** Read the article. What does each paragraph (1–4) talk about? Write the words in the reading. One is extra.

Art   Books and Comics   Clothing
Electronics   Food and More

C **Scan for details.** Match the items (1–6) with the place(s) where you can buy them (a–e). Some items may have more than one answer.

1. affordable clothes _____
2. a cell phone _____
3. expensive clothes _____
4. a traditional noodle soup _____
5. souvenirs _____
6. items for the home _____

a. Dongdaemun Market
b. Gangnam
c. Insadong
d. Namdaemun Market
e. Yongsan Market

D **Scan for details.** Write a number or word next to each place. If a number or word is not given, write *NG*.

The number of...

1. department stores in Gangnam: _____
2. malls in Dongdaemun Market: _____
3. stores in Dongdaemun Market: _____
4. stores in Yongsan Market: _____
5. places to eat in Namdaemun Market: _____
6. shops in Insadong: _____

E In your city, what are the best stores or neighborhoods to shop for the things in **B**? With a partner, make a shopping guide for visitors. Share it with the class.

ON SALE IN SEOUL

Are you planning to visit Seoul? South Korea's capital city has thousands of stores, so give yourself a day or more to go shopping. Here are some things you can buy:

1. _____

Need something to wear? Seoul has a lot of interesting places to shop for clothes. Department stores in the Gangnam neighborhood sell the latest fashions,[1] but they are expensive. For something more affordable, visit Dongdaemun Market. This large shopping area has over 20 malls and more than 25,000 smaller stores. Remember to bring cash and a shopping bag to hold all your items!

2. _____

Yongsan Market is the place to go for a new computer, phone, or camera. It has 5,000 stores and many items are on sale.

3. _____

Like Dongdaemun, Namdaemun Market is very large and has a lot of shops. These shops sell clothing, items for the home, and many other things—all at affordable prices. Namdaemun is also famous for its food, and there are many places to eat. Most sell traditional Korean dishes, including *kalguksu*—a delicious noodle soup.

4. _____

Looking for a souvenir[2] to take home? Visit Insadong, a beautiful, old neighborhood. Many shops sell traditional Korean drawings and other kinds of art. Some items are expensive, but many are affordable.

[1] *The latest fashions* are the most popular clothes of a certain time.
[2] A *souvenir* is something you buy on a trip to remember a place.

Outdoor food stalls like this one are common in Namdaemun.

4 GRAMMAR

A Turn to page 200. Complete the exercises. Then do **B–D** below.

Quantifiers with Affirmative and Negative Statements		
	Count nouns	**Noncount nouns**
	Do you have **any** friends?	Do you have **any** money?
Affirmative	Yes, I have **a lot of** / **many** friends. **some** friends.	Yes, I have **a lot of** money. **some** money.
Negative	No, I don't have **a lot of** / **many** friends. **any** friends.	No, I don't have **a lot of** / **much** money. **any** money.

B Make the sentences true for you. Circle a verb and then use a quantifier.

1. I (buy) / don't buy _____a lot of_____ clothing online.

2. I have / don't have _____ expensive shoes.

3. I wear / don't wear _____ jewelry.

4. I read / don't read _____ magazines.

5. I drink / don't drink _____ soda.

6. I spend / don't spend _____ money on souvenirs when I travel.

7. I have / don't have _____ video games at home.

8. I buy / don't buy _____ music online.

C 🔁 Ask a partner about his or her answers in **B**. Ask a question with *any.* Then ask one follow-up question. Are you and your partner similar or different?

> Do you buy any clothing online?

> No, I like to try things on.

D 👥 Share one way you and your partner are alike and one way you are different with the class.

5 WRITING

A 🔁 Read the paragraph. Answer the questions with a partner.

1. Where is the writer's favorite place to shop?

2. What kind of store is it?

3. Why is this store her favorite? Give two reasons.

My favorite place to shop is Uniqlo. It is a popular clothing store. I like this store for two reasons. **First**, a lot of their clothes are affordable. In a department store, I can only buy one pair of jeans. At Uniqlo, I can buy two or three. And the store always has things on sale! I'm a student and I don't have much money, so this is important. **Second**, Uniqlo's clothes are casual but nice. Many things are good for school and work. **For these reasons**, Uniqlo is my favorite place to shop.

B Answer the questions in **A** about your favorite place to shop. For each reason you give, explain it with an extra sentence or two. Then use your notes and the example to help you write your own paragraph.

C 🔁 Exchange your writing with a partner. Read his or her paragraph.

1. Are there any mistakes? If yes, circle them.

2. Answer the questions in **A** about your partner's writing. Do you know this store? Do you like it? Why or why not?

3. Return the paper to your partner. Make corrections to your own paragraph.

6 COMMUNICATION

A 🔁 Read about Jessie. Then describe her apartment with a partner.

Jessie is a 22-year-old university exchange student. She's living in your country for one year. She lives in a small apartment near her school. This is her apartment.

> Jessie doesn't have much furniture.

B 🔁 Jessie's parents want to visit her. Help Jessie prepare for her parents' visit. Work with a partner.

• What does her apartment have?

• What does her apartment need? Make a list.

• Where can she buy these things? Put your ideas on the list.

Things Jessie needs	Place to shop

> She needs some chairs. She can buy them at a department store.

C 🔺 Compare your list with another pair's list.

1 STORYBOARD

A Lisa and Eva are roommates. Look at the pictures and work with a partner to complete the conversations. More than one answer is possible for most blanks.

B Practice the conversations with a partner. Then change roles and practice again.

2 SEE IT AND SAY IT

A 🔄 Describe a person in the picture below to your partner. Don't say the person's name. Your partner guesses the person.

> This person has long hair and...

B 🔄 Talk about the picture with a partner.

- Where are the people?
- What are they doing?
- Which people are meeting for the first time? How do you know?
- Ask one question about the picture.

C 🔄 Choose one pair or group of people. With a partner, role-play a conversation of five to six sentences between the people.

> Hi, I'm Felipe.

> Hi, Felipe. Nice to meet you. My name is...

3 ODD WORD OUT

A   Look at the words. Circle the one that is different in each group.

1. nervous   embarrassed   angry   (happy)
2. (grapes)   carrots   onions   lettuce
3. red   gray   (curly)   black
4. cheese   yogurt   milk   (orange juice)
5. heavy   (short)   (slim)   thin
6. point at   bark at   wave to   (talk to)
7. (Japan)   Portuguese   Chinese   (English)

B   Compare and explain your answers with a partner.

> For number 1, happy is different. It's a good feeling. Nervous, embarrassed, and angry are bad feelings.

4 DO YOU EVER...?

A   Read each question. Answer *Yes* or *No*. Then write a sentence to give some extra information. Use the correct pronouns for the underlined words.

1. Do <u>you</u> give <u>your mom</u> flowers?

   Yes. I give her flowers on her birthday.

2. Does <u>your mom</u> speak to <u>your dad</u> in English?

   No She is

3. Do <u>you</u> eat <u>vegetables</u>?

   Yes I did

4. Do <u>your friends</u> send <u>you</u> text messages?

   Yes I did

5. Does <u>your instructor</u> give <u>you and your classmates</u> homework?

   Yes a lot of homowrk.

6. Do <u>you and your friends</u> give <u>your homework</u> to your instructor late?

   No I lot is hom

B   Ask your partner the questions in **A**. Listen to his or her answers. Then ask your partner one more question.

> Does your mom speak to your dad in English?

> Does he understand English?

> No, she always speaks to him in Spanish.

> No, not really.

5 LISTENING: THE PERFECT DIET?

A 🔊 Tino and Mary are talking about Tino's diet. Listen and circle your answers.
CD 1 Track 23

1. Which sentence is true?

   a. Mary thinks Tino eats too much.
   b. Tino is worried about his health.
   c. Mary thinks Tino's diet is too unhealthy.
   d. Tino is worried about Mary's health.

2. What is Tino NOT eating?

   a. protein
   b. vegetables
   c. fruit
   d. vitamins

B 🔊 Listen again. Which foods can he eat? Check the boxes. **CD1 Track 23**

C 🔄 Is Tino's diet healthy? Why or why not? Tell a partner.

6 TALK ABOUT...

A 👥 Get into a group of three people. Follow the steps below.

1. One person chooses a topic from the list and says it to the group.

   • your hobbies
   • why you are learning English
   • your favorite music
   • a country you want to visit

   • your favorite TV show
   • your favorite food
   • your best friend
   • something you don't like

   > My topic is "your hobbies."

   > What do you do for fun?

2. Each person in the group asks the first person a question about the topic. That person answers each question.

3. Take turns and repeat steps 1 and 2 for each topic.

VACATION

Look at the photo. Answer the questions.

1 What is this place like?

2 Do you want to go to this place?

3 What is a popular place for vacation in your country?

UNIT GOALS

1 Talk about weather conditions

2 Give and respond to advice

3 Talk about things you do on vacation

4 Discuss places you want to visit

Climbers relax in hammocks 40 meters off the ground in Monte Piana, Italy.

Santa Cruz, Portugal

1 **VIDEO** Imersão (Immersion)

A ▶ Read the list of places below. You are going to see scenes of Portugal. Watch the video and circle the places you see.

a forest	a market	a shopping mall
old buildings	new buildings	a mountain
the ocean	a bus	a soccer field
a movie theater	a beach	a town square

B Would you like to go on vacation in this country? Why or why not? Tell a partner.

C Think about the places in the video. With your partner, write three activities you can do in this country. Which is your favorite? Share your ideas with the class.

2 VOCABULARY

A Work with a partner. Study the information below about the region of Orellana, Ecuador. Then circle the correct words to describe the weather there now.

Orellana, Ecuador: current weather
January 28, 10:05 AM

20°C
Mostly cloudy

Wind: **calm**
Today's high: 31°C

Later today:
2 PM		Very **rainy**
6 PM		**Sunny** and **hot**
10 PM		**Clear** and **comfortable**

hot
warm
comfortable
chilly
cold
freezing

foggy

rainy

snowy

sunny

windy

i We often use a form of *be* with these weather words:
The sun is bright.
It's foggy today.

However, you can use *snow* and *rain* as verbs without *be:*
It snows / rains a lot here.
It's raining / snowing now.

1. Right now, it's raining / very windy / cloudy / sunny and it's warm / cold.

2. Today's high / low temperature is 31 degrees Celsius (88 degrees Fahrenheit). That's hot / comfortable / chilly.

B Draw a weather report for your city. Use the example above as a guide. How is the weather in your city the same as or different from Orellana's weather?

Orellana, Ecuador

3 LISTENING

A 🔊 **Pronunciation: Stress in multi-syllable words.** Practice saying the words aloud. Then listen and repeat. **CD 1 Track 24**

1. Noun: **rain**   2. Adjective: **rainy**   3. Verb: **raining**

B 🔊 **Pronunciation: Stress in multi-syllable words.** Read and listen to the sentences. Underline the stressed syllable in each bolded word. **CD 1 Track 25**

1. It's **chilly** this morning.   3. What's the **temperature** outside?
2. It's too **windy** for a picnic.   4. Are you on **vacation**?

C 🔊 **Listen for details.** Sam Ford is a weather reporter. He's interviewing Sofia. Where is Sofia, and what is she doing? Listen and circle the correct answers. **CD 1 Track 26**

1. Sofia is in the city center / the park right now.

2. There are about 2,000 / 20,000 people.

3. Sofia is from Mexico / Brazil.

4. It's 11:45 / 11:55 PM on New Year's Eve.

5. She's running a race of 3.1 / 5 kilometers.

D 🔊 Listen. How is the weather right now? Circle your answers and write in the temperature. **CD 1 Track 27**

Current temperature: 32 degrees F / 0 degrees C.

E 💬 Discuss the questions with a partner.

1. How's the weather in your city during the winter?

2. Do you ever exercise outside in the winter? How about in the summer? What weather do you like to exercise in?

3. Are there special runs like the one from the audio in your city? When are they?

Would you exercise in this weather?

4 SPEAKING

A 🔊 Read the conversation and listen. Then complete the conversation with the words in the box. **CD 1 Track 28**

foggy	pants	shorts
Los Angeles	San Francisco	warm

KYLE: There! All finished!

JULIET: Wait a minute.... You're going to San Francisco, right?

KYLE: Yeah. See? I have T-shirts, _shorts_, and my sandals.... I'm so excited!

JULIET: But, Kyle, San Francisco is cold and _foggy_ in the summer.

KYLE: Really? But San Francisco is in California! It's always sunny there!

JULIET: No, it's not. _Los Angeles_ is _warm_ and sunny, but not _San Francisco_.

KYLE: Oh...

JULIET: You should take some sweaters and long _pants_, too.

KYLE: Oh, OK. Good idea.

B 🗣 Practice the conversation with a partner.

SPEAKING STRATEGY

C 🗣 With a partner, choose a situation (1–4) below and create a short role play. Do steps 1 and 2. Then switch roles. Use the Useful Expressions to help you.

1. Your partner wants to drive to a party. It's snowing hard, and the roads aren't safe.

2. Your partner wants to have a picnic on Saturday. The weather forecast is for rain all day.

3. You and your partner are at the beach. It's very hot and sunny. Your partner sunburns easily, and he or she wants to go swimming right away.

4. Your partner wants to go jogging on a cold day. He or she is wearing shorts and a T-shirt.

1. **Student A:** Give advice to your partner in two different ways.

2. **Student B:** Refuse the advice the first time. Then accept it.

Useful Expressions		
Giving advice		
Advice	Accepting	Refusing
(I think) you should take a sweater.	Good idea. OK, I will.	Really? I don't think so. Really? I'd rather not.
I don't think you should drive. You shouldn't drive.	You're probably right.	Really? I think I'll be OK.

> It's snowing outside. I don't think you should drive.

> Really? I think I'll be OK. I'm a good driver.

> But the roads aren't safe.

5 GRAMMAR

A Turn to page 201. Complete the exercises. Then do **B–D** below.

Connecting Ideas with *but, or,* and *so*	
It's freezing in Moscow, **but** it's warm in Rio.	Use *but* to show an opposite idea or contrast.
We can go to the beach, **or** we can visit the zoo.	Use *or* to give choices.
It's raining, **so** we're not having a picnic today.	Use *so* to introduce a result.

B Oona is introducing you to her city. Read the sentences and complete them with *but, or,* and *so.*

MY CITY: CHIANG MAI, THAILAND

Doi Suthep, Chiang Mai, Thailand

1. I like to show visitors beautiful places,
   _____but_____ I take them to Mount Inthanon.

2. During the day, the Old City is famous for its
   temples, _____so_____ at night it's famous for a
   large night market.

3. Sometimes it's crowded in the city, _____and_____
   I go to Nong Buak Hard Public Park to relax.

4. For a fancy night out, I go for drinks at the
   Le Meridien Hotel, _____and_____ I have dinner at
   The Riverside restaurant.

5. City life is expensive, _____but_____ there are plenty
   of cheap things to do, too. I like to go for a walk in
   Doi Suthep-Pui National Park.

6. Just outside my city, you can take an elephant
   _____or_____ boat tour of the jungle.

C 🗣 Now imagine a visitor is coming to your city. What will you tell him or her? Use the sentences in **B** as a guide. Complete the sentences below with your own ideas. Work with a partner.

1. I like to show visitors beautiful places, _____.
2. During the day, _____ is famous for _____, _____ at
   night _____.
3. Sometimes it's crowded in the city, _____.
4. For a fancy night out, _____.
5. City life is expensive, _____ there are plenty of free things to do, too. I like to

   _____.
6. Just outside my city, you can _____.

D 👥 Share your answers with another pair. Choose the two best tips from both lists and share them with the class.

6 COMMUNICATION

A 💬 Interview your partner. Complete the survey with his or her answers. Check (✓) the answers.

Vacation Survey

1. I usually take a vacation in the
   _____.
   ☐ spring   ☐ fall
   ☐ summer   ☐ winter

2. I like _____ weather.
   ☐ hot
   ☐ warm
   ☐ cold
   ☐ other (your idea): _____

3. I like to _____ on vacation.
   ☐ relax
   ☐ exercise
   ☐ see things
   ☐ other: _____

4. What are your favorite activities?

☐ swimming

☐ skiing

☐ surfing

☐ hiking

☐ golfing

☐ mountain biking

☐ other: _____

B Read about the places below and choose one for your partner's vacation.

Cape Town, South Africa

Weather:
- In spring and summer (September–March), it's warm.
- The fall and winter months are chilly, and it rains.

Activities:
This coastal city has beautiful mountains and lovely beaches. They're great for:
- hiking.
- surfing.
- swimming.
- relaxing.
- waterskiing.

Las Vegas, US

Weather:
- Sunny days, comfortable evenings all year.
- In summer, it's 100°F / 38°C.

Activities:
- The casinos, nightlife, and restaurants are popular.
- There are many swimming pools and golf courses.
- Beautiful mountains are just outside of the city for hiking and for skiing and snowboarding in winter.

Sapporo, Japan

Weather:
- There's low humidity all year.
- Winters are cold with a lot of snow.
- July and August are dry and beautiful.

Activities:
- Skiing is popular in winter.
- Summer is great for camping, hiking, and mountain biking.
- The popular Sapporo Snow Festival is held in February.

C 💬 Tell your partner your suggestion. Explain your reasons. Does your partner like your suggestion?

1 VOCABULARY

A With a partner, match the vacation activities (a–h) with the photos.

a. pack your suitcase   d. go sightseeing   g. post photos online

b. check in to your hotel   e. get a passport   h. unpack

c. buy a plane ticket   f. take photos

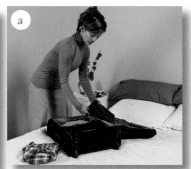

B Answer the questions with your partner.

1. Which activities in **A** do you do before your trip? while on vacation? after your trip?

2. Do you have a passport?

3. On vacation, do you like to go sightseeing? Do you take a lot of photos?

4. Imagine you can go anywhere on vacation. Where do you want to go?

5. Do you ever post photos from your vacations? Do you have any on your phone now? If yes, show one to your partner.

> I don't have a passport. I need to get one.

Word Bank
go on vacation = go on a trip
Opposites
check in to ↔ check out of (a hotel)
pack ↔ unpack

2 LISTENING

A 🔁 **Infer information.** Look at the photos. What are the people doing? Tell a partner.

B 🔊 **Listen for gist.** Listen to three conversations. Match each conversation (1, 2, or 3) to a photo. One photo is extra. **CD 1 Track 29**

C 🔊 **Listen for context.** Look at your answers (1, 2, 3) in **B**. What are the people doing? Listen. You will hear three possible answers. Circle the correct answer. **CD 1 Track 30**

1. A   B   (C)
2. (A)   B   C
3. A   (B)   C

D 🔊 **Make predictions; Listen for details.** Read the three dialogs. Guess the missing words. Then listen again and check your answers. **CD 1 Track 29**

1. **A:** _May_ I see your passport, please?
   B: _Sure_, here you go.
2. **A:** _Can_ you _take_ our _Picture_, please?
   B: _Sure_.
3. **A:** _Can_ I see a credit card and some form of _ID_, please?
   B: _of course_

3 READING

A  **Understand the gist; Make predictions.** Read the title and first paragraph of the article. Answer the questions with a partner.

1. Many travelers have a problem. What is it?

2. Do you ever have this problem?

3. Guess: Think of one tip (helpful idea) the article will talk about.

B **Identify main ideas.** Read the article. Write each tip below in the correct paragraph (1–5) of the reading.

Don't bring books.

Choose simple colors.

Make a list.

Use plastic bags.

Wear your warm clothes on the plane.

C **Scan for details.** Read the questions. Then read the article again and take notes on the answers.

Why should you…

1. make a list before you pack?

2. bring a tablet?

3. buy magazines or books at the airport?

4. pack clothes of certain colors? Which colors are best?

5. wear your warm clothes on the plane?

6. use plastic bags?

D  Ask and answer the questions in **C** with a partner.

E  In your opinion, which tip is the best? Can you think of any other tips? Tell a partner.

HOW TO PACK
FOR YOUR NEXT TRIP

Going on vacation is fun, but packing usually is not. "What should I bring?" travelers often ask. Many people are unsure and pack too much. Then they have to carry a heavy[1] suitcase or pay extra money for it at the airport. How can you pack your things in one easy-to-carry bag? Here are some helpful tips from travel writers Annie Fitzsimmons and Jared Gottlieb:

1. _____. When you travel, you only *need* a few things: your passport, credit cards, cell phone, and certain clothes (a suit for work, a sweater for cool weather, shorts for hot weather). What are these things? Make a list. Then pack only the important items.

2. _____. Do you plan to read on the trip? Leave books at home. They're heavy. If you want to read, bring your tablet, or buy magazines or books at the airport. When you're done, you can leave them on the plane or at the hotel.

3. _____. Bring mostly white, black, gray, tan, and blue clothes and shoes. These colors are easy to mix and match.[2] By doing this, you can pack fewer items.

4. _____. Are you going someplace chilly? If yes, wear some of your warm clothes—like sweaters, jackets, or boots—on the plane. These things take up a lot of room in your suitcase and make it heavy.

5. _____. Use these bags to organize[3] the items in your suitcase. Put things like your toothbrush, soap, and shampoo in one bag, underwear and socks in another, shirts in another, and so on. By doing this, you use less space in your suitcase. It also makes it easier to unpack!

[1] A *heavy* object weighs a lot.
[2] If you *mix and match* two or more things, you put them together so they look good.
[3] If you *organize* things, you put them together in a neat, orderly way.

Travelers wait for a train in Berlin, Germany

4 GRAMMAR

A Turn to page 202. Complete the exercises. Then do **B** and **C** below.

	Possessive Adjectives	Possessive Pronouns	*belong to*
	It's **my** passport.	It's **mine**.	It **belongs to me**.
	your	**yours**.	**you**.
Whose passport is this?	**her**	**hers**.	**her**.
	his	**his**.	**him**.
	our	**ours**.	**us**.
	their	**theirs**.	**them**.

B Make two wishes about travel—places you want to go or things you want to do. Write each wish on a small piece of paper.

I want to _____.

I want to _____.

> ### Travel wishes
> Get a passport
> Go on a cruise
> Go on a safari in Africa
> Go to another city or country
> Live in another country
> My idea: _____

C Work in a small group. Follow the steps below.

1. Mix all of the group's wishes together. Put them face down on the desk.

2. One person begins. Take a piece of paper and read it aloud. Then ask: *Whose wish is this?* Try to guess.

3. When you find the person, ask a question about his or her wish.

4. Repeat steps 1–3. Talk about all your wishes.

A: *I want to go to Egypt.* Whose wish is this? Is it yours, Oscar?

B: No, it's not mine. Maybe it's hers—Bianca's.

C: Yes, it belongs to me!

A: Why do you want to go to Egypt?

C: I want to see the pyramids!

5 WRITING

A Read the social media conversation on the next page. Min is posting about her vacation. Answer the questions with a partner.

1. Where is Min going? Where is this place?
2. What happens to Min at the airport?
3. Where is she staying?
4. How's the weather?
5. Lisa gives Min some advice. What does Lisa say?

B On your own, do the following.

1. Think of a place you want to go on vacation. Where is it? Where are you staying? How's the weather there?

2. On the top of a piece of paper, write your name and complete the sentence below.

   I'm checking in at the airport for my trip to _____!

MIN   I'm checking in at the airport for my trip to Palau!
24 hours * Like

 YUKI   Where is that exactly?
24 hours * Like

 MIN   It's an island near the Philippines.
24 hours * Like

 LISA   Have fun! Take lots of photos and make
sure to post them!
24 hours * Like

 MIN   Thanks, Lisa! Oh no! My suitcase
is too heavy, so I have to pay extra!
24 hours * Like

 LISA   I always pack too much, too! ☺
23 hours * Like

 YUKI   Are you there yet?
3 hours * Like

 MIN   Yeah. I'm checking in to my hotel.
It's near the beach!
3 hours * Like

 YUKI   How's the weather?
3 hours * Like

 MIN   It's raining right now, but it's warm. It's beautiful here!
3 hours * Like

 LISA   You should go swimming with the jellyfish!
3 hours * Like

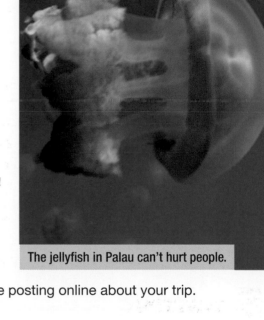

The jellyfish in Palau can't hurt people.

C 🔘 Work in a group of three. Sit in a circle. Imagine you are posting online about your trip.
Follow the steps below.

1. Give your paper from **B** to the person on your right.

2. Read the sentence on the paper you get. Write a reply below it. Look at the example for ideas.

3. Then repeat steps 1 and 2. Continue for five minutes, "posting" about your vacations.

4. At the end, get your original paper back. Make corrections to your partners' writing.
Check for the proper possessive adjectives and pronouns.

6 COMMUNICATION

A 🔘 Ask a new partner the questions below about his or her vacation from Writing.

1. Where are you going?   3. How's the weather?

2. Where are you staying?   4. What do you like most about the place?

B 🔘 Repeat **A** with two new partners. Whose vacation is the most interesting? Why?

5 HEROES

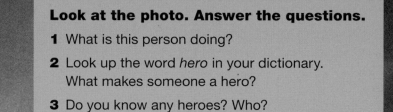

Look at the photo. Answer the questions.

1 What is this person doing?

2 Look up the word *hero* in your dictionary. What makes someone a hero?

3 Do you know any heroes? Who?

UNIT GOALS

1 Talk about interesting people and their jobs

2 Give, agree, and disagree with opinions

3 Explain why you admire someone

4 Narrate a story

Journalists and photographers travel to dangerous areas to share important stories with the world.

Alex Zanardi competes in a handcycle race.

1 VIDEO Touch the Sky

[handwritten: campeat (أقباس)]

A Review the meaning of the words in the box with your instructor. Then look at the photo and read about Alex Zanardi. Try to complete the sentences with the words in the box. Two words are extra.

present		past
is	→	was
lose	→	lost
race	→	raced

> arms   bikes   cars   legs

Alex Zanardi is a Formula 1 race car driver from Italy. In the past, he raced cars. Then he was in an accident. He lost his ___legs___. Now he races ___arms___.

B ▶ Watch the video. Check your answers in **A**.

C ▶ Watch again. Complete the quotes from Alex Zanardi.

1. (0:27): "Even the greatest d_____ can be turned into your greatest v_*defeat*_."
2. (2:51): "I'm a l_*Alex Zanardi*_ person because at the age of 47, things are not over yet."

D 🔁 Answer the questions with a partner.

1. Look again at sentences 1 and 2 in **C**. What do they mean? Explain in your own words.
2. Do you agree with sentence 1?

Will Steger with his sled dogs

2 VOCABULARY

A 🔗 Look at the photo and caption. Who is this person? What is he doing? Tell a partner.

B 🔗 Read about Will Steger. Name two places he has visited and two things that he does or has done. Which of the jobs or activities are interesting to you? Tell your partner.

Who he is	What he does
Will Steger is an **explorer**.	He was the **leader** on a 1,200 mile (1,931 km) trip between Russia and Canada.
He is a **traveler**.	He was the first person to travel to both the North and South Poles by dogsled.
He is an **ambassador** for the planet.	He is a popular **speaker**. He talks about the changes in weather on the poles and around the world.
He is a **writer**.	He is the **author** of four books, including *Saving the Earth*.
He is a **teacher**.	He is the **founder** of the Steger Wilderness Center. He wants **educators** and **scientists** to come to the center. They can learn about the earth.

C 🔗 Tell a partner about one or more famous people. Use three of the words in the chart below.

-ian	-or	-ist	-er
music**ian**	direct**or**	activ**ist**	research**er**
physic**ian**	doct**or**	journal**ist**	teach**er**
politic**ian**	instruct**or**	scient**ist**	travel**er**

Jane Goodall is a famous scientist and researcher. She's also a popular speaker. She studies chimpanzees.

3 LISTENING

Canada

Costa Rica

Iceland

Antarctica

A Look at the shaded places on the map. What do you know about these places?

B 🔊 **Infer information.** A radio announcer is interviewing Alejandro about his job. Listen to the interview and answer the question. **CD 1 Track 32**

Where in the world is Alejandro? Circle it on the map.

C 🔊 **Listen for gist.** Listen again. What job(s) does Alejandro do? Circle your answer(s). **CD 1 Track 32**

doctor   journalist   scientist   photographer   explorer   ski instructor

D 🔊 **Listen for details.** Listen again. What does Alejandro say?
Complete the sentences by circling the correct words. **CD 1 Track 32**

1. Sometimes my camera breaks / freezes.

2. Today it's −13 / −30 degrees.

3. I was born in Costa Rica / Canada.

4. This place is very quiet / nice.

5. I write for a newspaper / online.

E ⟳ Discuss the questions with a partner.

1. Why is Alejandro's job dangerous?

2. Is his job interesting to you? Why or why not?

3. Can you name any other dangerous jobs?

4 SPEAKING

A 🔊 Listen to the conversation. Then follow the steps (1, 2) and answer the questions (3). **CD 1 Track 33**

1. Find a word that means *not afraid*.
2. Find a word that means *a movie that shows real events*.
3. Do Kurt and Maggie like the movie? How do you know?

KURT: Hey, Maggie. What movie are you watching tonight?

MAGGIE: It's a documentary. It's called *Man on Wire*. It's my second time watching it.

KURT: *Man on Wire*... hmm....

MAGGIE: Do you know it?

KURT: Yeah, I do. It's a great movie.

MAGGIE: I agree. The guy in the movie was really brave.

KURT: Oh, I know. And it was in New York. I love New York City!

MAGGIE: Me, too. Hey, do you want to watch the movie with me?

KURT: Again? Well... sure. Why not?

B 🔁 Practice the conversation with a partner.

SPEAKING STRATEGY

C Complete the chart with information about two movies you like.

Name of movie	Actor(s) in movie	Words that describe movie

D 👥 In a group, talk about your movies. Use the Useful Expressions and the example to help you.

A: I think *Frozen* is a good movie.

B: Yeah, I agree. It's really fun.

C: Really? I don't think so.

B: Why do you say that?

C: I think the story is kind of boring.

Useful Expressions		
Agreeing or disagreeing with an opinion		
Statement: I think *Man on Wire* is a good movie.		**Follow-up questions**
Agreeing	I think so, too. I agree. Yeah, you're right.	What do you like about it?
Disagreeing	Really? I don't think so. Sorry, but I disagree. I don't really agree.	Why do you say that?
Speaking tip		
You can agree with a negative statement by saying *Me neither*. A: I don't like that movie. B: Me neither.		

5 GRAMMAR

am / is →	**was**
am not / isn't →	**wasn't**
are →	**were**
aren't →	**weren't**

A Turn to page 203. Complete the exercises. Then do **B–F** below.

The Simple Past Tense with *be*		
Affirmative and Negative Statements		
Subject	***was / were***	
I / He / She / It	**was / wasn't**	brave.
We / You / They	**were / weren't**	

Yes / No Questions			**Answers**
Was / Were	**Subject**		
Were	you	brave?	Yes, I **was**. / No, I **wasn't**.
Was	she		Yes, she **was**. / No, she **wasn't**.

Wh- Questions				**Answers**
***Wh-* word**	***was / were***	**Subject**		
When	**was**	he	born?	**Last** year. / A year **ago**. / **In** 2015.

B Use the words in the box to complete the chart. Pay attention to the verb forms in the chart.

ago	They
in	was
She	weren't
last	

Subject	***be***	
I / He / _____ / It	_____ / wasn't	there _____ 2007.
		on TV _____ night.
You / We / _____	were / _____	famous two years _____.

C Read about these explorers. Complete the sentences with simple past tense forms of *be*.

1963

Who (1.) _____ the first woman to fly in space?

Her name (2.) _____ Valentina Tereshkova.

She (3.) _____ Russian.

There (4.) _____ any other women in space for 19 years.

1980

Peng Jiamu (5.) _____ a famous scientist.

He (6.) _____ an explorer in the Lop Nur Desert of China.

He (7.) _____ lost in the desert in 1980.

His team members (8.) _____ able to find him. He was never seen again.

D Complete the chart with your birth year (1) and birthplace (2). Then complete 3–5 with information that was true about yourself *three years ago*.

	1. Birth year	2. Birthplace	3. Age	4. School	5. Best friend
Example	2001	Santiago	15	Colegio	Cesar
You					

E Interview two classmates. Ask them questions and complete the chart on p. 68 with their information.

> Where were you born?

> In the Dominican Republic.

F Share your information with another partner.

> This is Juan David. He was born in Santo Domingo. Three years ago, he was 15 years old.

> Were you born in Santo Domingo?

6 COMMUNICATION

A Read the headings in the chart. Then think of famous people you know and complete the chart. The people can be from the past or present. Share your answers with a partner.

Entertainers*	
Leaders	
Writers	
Explorers	
Activists	
(Other: your idea)	

* = singers, actors, musicians, etc.

B Use your information in **A** and follow the steps below.

1. You are going to have a dinner party. You can invite four famous people from the past or present.

2. Complete the chart with the names and jobs of the people you want to invite.

3. List your reasons for inviting them.

1. **Person:** **Job:** **Reason:**	
2. **Person:** **Job:** **Reason:**	
3. **Person:** **Job:** **Reason:**	
4. **Person:** **Job:** **Reason:**	

C Get into a group of three people. Compare your answers in **B**. Explain your choices. Together, make one list of four people to invite to the party.

> I think we should invite Junko Tabei. She was the first woman to climb Mount Everest.

> I agree. Let's invite her.

LESSON B PERSONAL HEROES

Knicole Colón: astronomer
(a scientist who studies space)
and National Geographic Explorer

As a kid, who was your role-model?
At age 12, I saw the movie *Contact*. In the movie, there's a woman named Ellie. She works as an astronomer, and she's looking for life on other planets. She's very smart. She's brave, too. She travels to space alone. She was only a character in a movie, but I really looked up to her! I also really admire the astronomer Galileo Galilei. He's my hero, too.

1 VOCABULARY

A Read the definition. Then circle the words that can complete the sentence below. Look up any new words.

A *role-model* is someone you *admire*. You think the person is great. You want to be like the person. What words describe a role-model?

Word Bank
admire = look up to (someone)
role-model = hero

A role-model is a _____ person.

brave	confused	hardworking	nervous
confident	generous	kind	smart / intelligent

B Read the interview with Knicole Colón. Then answer the questions with a partner.

1. What does Knicole Colón do?

2. As a kid, who was her hero?

3. Why did Knicole look up to this person?

4. Who else does Knicole admire?

C Complete the sentences. Use words in **A** to describe the person.

I admire _____. I look up to this person because _____.

2 LISTENING

Jack Andraka is an inventor.

Lydia Ko is a golf player.

A Look at the words in the Word Bank. Then read the photo captions. What do these two people do? Tell a partner.

Word Bank
cancer = a very serious disease
die = to stop living
invent = to be first to make something
tool = a handheld item used for work

B **Listen for gist.** Listen to a profile of each person. Check the best title for each. **CD 1 Track 34**

1. ☑ Jack Andraka: Brave Teenage Doctor

   ☐ Jack Andraka: Smart Scientist

2. ☐ Lydia Ko: Hardworking Athlete

   ☑ Lydia Ko: Generous Golf Player

C **Listen for details.** Listen again. Complete the sentences with a word or number. **CD 1 Track 34**

1. When Jack was _____, his friend died of cancer.

2. Jack was very _b̲r̲a̲v̲e̲_.

3. At age _____, he invented a _____.

4. It helps doctors find certain cancers _____.

5. Lydia started playing golf at age _____.

6. She practiced to be the _____.

7. By age _____, she was the number _____ women's golf player.

8. For years, golf was mostly a _____ sport. Now, more _____ want to play.

D Do you admire Jack and Lydia? Why or why not? Tell a partner.

3 READING

A  **Make predictions; Infer information.**
Look at the photos on the next page. Sanga Moses invented something. What is it? Tell a partner.

B **Read for details.** Read paragraphs 1 and 2. Then complete the sentences.

1. In Uganda, many people use _____ to cook.

2. This makes the air _____.

3. Many children don't go to _____.

4. Sanga Moses's company invented a new _____.

5. It changes extra or unused _____ parts into fuel.

C **Sequence events.** Read the first question and answer in the reading. Then put the events in order from 1 to 6.

_____ Sanga Moses decided to fix the problem.

_____ He talked to his sister.

_____ He stopped working at the bank.

_____ Sanga Moses visited his mother.

_____ He started Eco-Fuel Africa.

_____ She cried because she missed school to get wood.

D **Read for details.** Read the second question and answer in the reading. Complete the sentence and the four reasons.

Sanga Moses's invention is / isn't helping people.

1. Women are making _____.

2. The air is _____.

3. People are saving _____.

4. Girls can stay in _____.

E  Work with a partner. Use your answers in **B–D** to answer the questions.

1. What was the problem in Uganda?

2. What did Sanga Moses do about the problem?

3. Do you admire Sanga Moses? Why or why not?

ECO-FUEL AFRICA

One company is changing people's lives in Uganda.

In Uganda, many people use wood for fuel.[1] But using wood makes the air dirty. Also many children—usually girls—don't go to school. They spend hours getting the wood for cooking.

But now things are changing. Sanga Moses started a company called Eco-Fuel Africa. The company invented a new kind of oven. It changes extra or unused food parts into fuel. This kind of fuel is clean (unlike wood). Here, Sanga Moses answers two questions about his company.

Why did you start Eco-Fuel Africa?

Sanga Moses: In January 2009, I worked in a big bank in Kampala (the capital of Uganda). One day, I visited my mother in my home village. Going home, I met my 12-year-old sister on the road. She carried a lot of wood. My sister started crying. She didn't go to school that day because she walked for ten kilometers to get wood for my family. I was very unhappy about this. I wanted my sister to stay in school. That day, I decided to fix[2] this problem. I stopped working at the bank, and I started Eco-Fuel Africa.

Is Eco-Fuel Africa helping people?

Sanga Moses: Yes, I think so. For example, we have a group of 460 women. They use our ovens to make clean cooking fuel. Then they sell it. Each woman makes $150 a month in extra money. And about 115,000 people use our clean cooking fuel in Uganda. Today, the air is cleaner, and we are saving trees. And best of all, girls can stay in school.

[1]*Fuel* is something like wood or oil. People use fuel to make energy for cooking food and other activities.
[2]If something doesn't work and you *fix* it, you make it work.

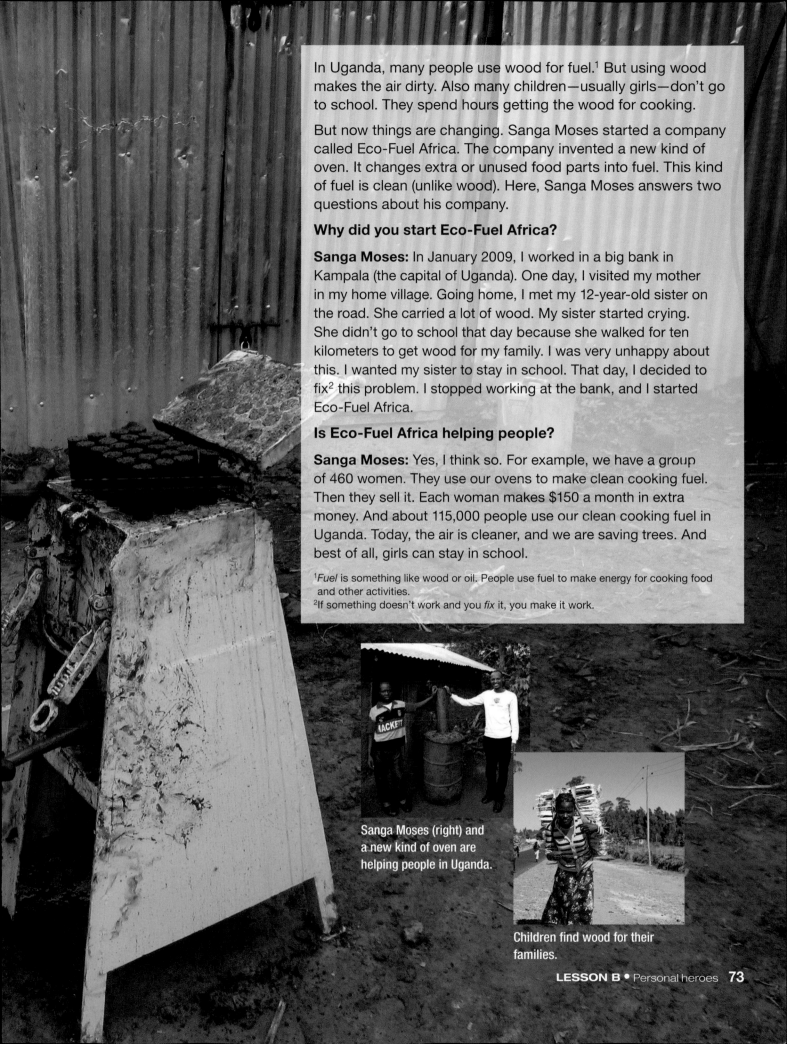

Sanga Moses (right) and a new kind of oven are helping people in Uganda.

Children find wood for their families.

4 GRAMMAR

A Turn to page 204. Complete the exercises. Then do **B–E** below.

The Simple Past: Affirmative and Negative Statements		
I / You / He / She / We / They	visit**ed** didn't visit	Tokyo.
I / You / He / She / We / They	start**ed** didn't start	a company.

move → mov**ed**

start → start**ed**

study → stud**ied**

stop → stop**ped**

B 🔊 **Pronunciation: Past tense -ed endings.**
Listen to these past tense verbs. Say each word with the speaker. Pay attention to the pronunciation of the -ed ending. **CD 1 Track 36**

/t/	/d/	/ɪd/
liked, stopped	moved, tried	visited, waited

C 🔊 🔄 **Pronunciation: Past tense -ed endings.** How is the -ed sound said in each verb? Listen and circle your answer. Then say the words with a partner. **CD 1 Track 37**

1. walked /t/ /ɪd/
2. started /d/ /ɪd/
3. wanted /d/ /ɪd/
4. returned /d/ /ɪd/
5. asked /t/ /ɪd/
6. cried /d/ /ɪd/
7. listened /d/ /ɪd/
8. needed /t/ /ɪd/
9. finished /t/ /ɪd/

D 🔄 Work with a partner. Complete Alec's story with simple past tense verbs. Then take turns reading the story aloud. Pay attention to pronunciation.

Help from a Stranger

There was a girl named Alyssa in my class. I (1. like) _____ her a lot. One day, I (2. invite) _____ her to have dinner with me at a restaurant.

At the end, I (3. ask) _____ the waiter for the check. I (4. offer) _____ to pay. I (5. look) _____ in my wallet, but I only had ten dollars. I (6. not have) _____ enough money!

I left the table. I (7. try) _____ to call my roommate. I (8. wait) _____, but my roommate (9. not answer) _____ his phone. I left a message and (10. explain) _____ my problem.

Just then, the door (11. open) _____. It was my waiter. He (12. hand) _____ me $40. I (13. promise) _____ to pay him back. He (14. reply) _____, "Don't worry about it." What a kind and generous guy!

E 🔄 Ask and answer the questions with a partner.

1. Where were Alec and Alyssa?
2. What happened after dinner?
3. When Alec realized his problem, what did he do?
4. Who helped Alec?
5. What did Alec promise?
6. What did the waiter reply?

5 WRITING

*196 507 6161
Nazillah ibrahimi*

A Read the paragraph. Complete the sentences with simple past tense verbs.

My Hero

My hero is my grandmother. I admire her a lot. She is very smart and hardworking. At age 35, she (1. start) _started_ her own business. She (2. own) _owned_ a small store. At first, she (3. not know) _knew_ a lot about business, but she (4. work) _worked_ hard, and she (5. learn) _learned_ fast. In time, her store (6. be) _be_ successful. She (7. hire) _hire_ five people. I also (8. help) _helped_ her in the summers. I (9. learn) _learned_ a lot about business from my grandmother. Now my grandmother is 74 years old. Two years ago, she (10. close) _closed_ her store, but she is still busy. She travels and she sees her friends. She is a great woman!

B Check your answers in **A** with a partner. Then answer the questions.

1. Who does the writer admire?
2. Why? What did the person do?
3. The writer uses adjectives to describe his hero. What are they?

C Who is your hero? Answer the questions in **B** about your person. Then use your notes and the model in **A** to help you write your own paragraph.

D Share your writing with a partner. Circle any mistakes and answer the questions in **B**. Then return the paper to your partner. Make corrections to your own paragraph.

6 COMMUNICATION

A Every year, there are three choices for the Hero of the Year award. Read about this year's three choices. Which person is your choice? Why?

Jason Yang, 30

Five years ago, Jason Yang started his own company. Today, he is a millionaire. This year he is giving ten poor children $10,000 each for college.

Amanda Garcia, 54

A month ago, there was a car fire near Amanda Garcia's house. A child was in the car. Amanda pulled the child from the car. She saved the little boy's life.

Logan Myers, 22

When he was 16, Logan Myers was in a car accident. Now he is in a wheelchair. This year, he climbed 3,776 meters to the top of Mount Fuji using special ropes. Now Logan is preparing for his next challenge: Mount Everest.

B Get into a group of three or four people. Explain your choice to the group. Then together choose one person to get the award. Explain your answer to the class.

> I admire Logan. He's very brave and...

6 THE MIND

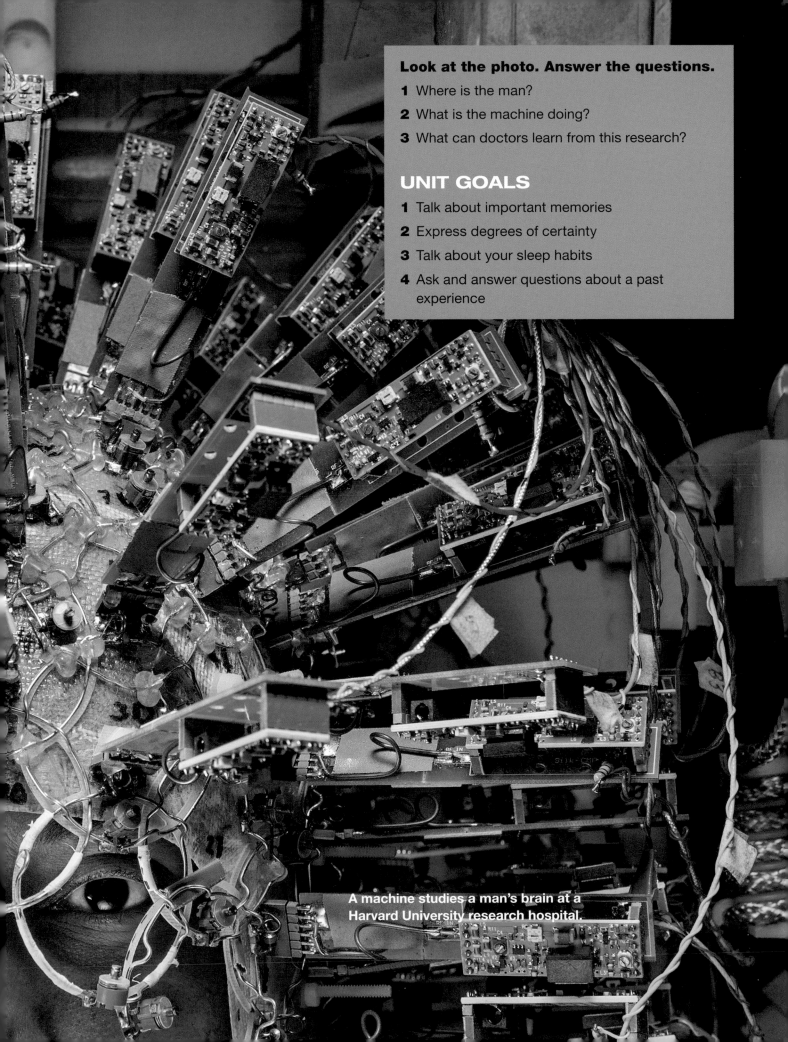

Look at the photo. Answer the questions.

1 Where is the man?

2 What is the machine doing?

3 What can doctors learn from this research?

UNIT GOALS

1 Talk about important memories

2 Express degrees of certainty

3 Talk about your sleep habits

4 Ask and answer questions about a past experience

A machine studies a man's brain at a Harvard University research hospital.

A man falls asleep on a city bus.

1 VIDEO The Sleep Test

A 🔁 Look at the Word Bank. Then ask a partner: Are you sleep deprived?

<table>
<tr><th>Word Bank</th></tr>
<tr><td>being sleep deprived = needing more sleep</td></tr>
</table>

B ▶ Watch the first 30 seconds of the video with the sound off. Circle the changes you see. Then watch with the sound on to check your answers.

the buildings disappear   the clouds get bigger

the bus changes color   the child runs toward the road

C ▶ Read the questions and review the meaning of the words in **bold** with your instructor. Then watch the whole video and write a word to complete each question.

1. Do you need an alarm _____ to **wake up**?

2. Do you **fall asleep** after _____ minutes in bed?

3. Do you drink a lot of _____ or energy drinks to **stay awake**?

D 🔁 Ask and answer the questions in **C** with a partner.

2 VOCABULARY

"Hi, I think I know you..."

A Read the sentences in the chart about memory. How many of them are true for you? Compare your answers with a partner's.

Word Bank
Opposites
remember ◄─────► forget
(to keep information in your mind)   (to not remember)

	Yes	No
1. I sometimes **forget** to do my homework.	☐	☐
2. When I leave the house, I never **forget** my house key.	☐	☐
3. I'm **good at remembering** people's names.	☐	☐
4. I **can** always **remember** my friends' birthdays.	☐	☐
5. I **have** an excellent **memory**.	☐	☐
6. Looking at old photos **brings back** many happy **memories**.	☐	☐
7. I **can** sing a song in English **from memory**.	☐	☐
8. **I'll never forget the day** I graduated from school.	☐	☐

B Complete these sentences with your own ideas. Discuss your answers with a partner.

1. I sometimes forget to _____.
2. When I leave the house, I never forget my _____.
3. I'm good at remembering _____.
4. I always remember _____ birthday(s).
5. I have a(n) _____ memory.
6. _____ brings back many happy memories.
7. I can _____ from memory.
8. I'll never forget the day I _____.

Word Bank
Words used to talk about memory
have a(n) excellent / sharp / good / bad / poor memory
a happy / good / sad / painful memory

> During the day, I sometimes forget to check my email.

> Not me! I check mine every 10 minutes!

3 LISTENING

A 💬 Are you good at remembering new words in English? Why or why not? Tell a partner.

B 🔊 **Listen for main ideas.** Listen to part of Galina and Tomo's conversation. Circle the correct answer to complete each sentence. **CD 1 Track 38**

1. They're talking about a _____.

   a. word   b. test   c. dictionary

2. Tomo is worried because _____.

   a. he thinks he did poorly   b. he just got a bad grade   c. he has a lot of homework

C 🔊 **Listen for details.** Listen to the entire conversation. Look at the pictures. Check (✓) the things Galina does. **CD 1 Track 39**

D 💬 Read these methods for learning new vocabulary in English. Which ones do you like? Discuss with a partner. How do you remember new words in English?

- Practice saying the new word again and again.

- Put important new words in places where you will see them during the day (on your laptop or on the bathroom mirror, for example). Every time you see the word, say it aloud.

- Exchange new information with the word. For example, for *beach*, ask a friend, *What's your favorite beach?*

- Make a sentence using the word. Use real people and facts from your life in the sentence.

- Listen to a story in English. At the same time, read the story in your own language.

- Your idea: _____.

If you travel to a country where people speak English, practice speaking with the people there.

4 SPEAKING

A 🔊 Listen to Mia and Justin's conversation. Where do you think they're going? What is Justin looking for? **CD 1 Track 40**

MIA: I'm so excited! Are you ready to go in?

JUSTIN: Um... just a minute. I can't find the tickets.

MIA: You're kidding!

JUSTIN: No, I'm not. I put them in my front pocket. See? They're not there.

MIA: Well, are they in your backpack?

JUSTIN: I don't think so.

MIA: Maybe you dropped them somewhere.

JUSTIN: Maybe. I'm not sure.

MIA: Oh, Justin. What are we going to do?

JUSTIN: Wait... hold on. I found them. They were in my *back* pocket.

MIA: Great! Let's go!

B 🗘 Practice the conversation with a partner.

SPEAKING STRATEGY

C 🗘 Read the questions below. Add your own question for each topic. Then take turns asking and answering the questions with a partner. Use the Useful Expressions in your answers.

Your instructor	Your partner
Is your instructor married? Does your instructor like vegetables? Your question: _____	Does your partner live near you? Does your partner like rap music? Your question: _____
Your school	**Public schools in the US**
Are there a lot of restaurants near your school? Is there a bus stop near your school? Your question: _____	Do students wear uniforms? Does the school year start in the fall? Your question: _____

Useful Expressions
Expressing degrees of certainty
Are they in your backpack?
Yes, they are. / No, they aren't. (very certain)
I think so. / I don't think so. (less certain)
Maybe. I'm not sure. (not very certain)
I have no idea. (= I don't know.)

5 GRAMMAR

A Turn to page 205. Complete the exercises. Then do **B**–**D** below.

The Simple Past: Affirmative and Negative Statements (Irregular Verbs)			
Subject	***did + not***	**Verb**	
I / You / He / She / We / They		forgot	her birthday.
	didn't	forget	

B 🔊 **Pronunciation: Irregular past tense verbs.** Practice saying the verb pairs in row A aloud. Then listen and repeat. Can you guess the pronunciation for the verbs in row B? Say them aloud. Then listen and repeat. **CD 1 Track 41**

Row A	forget / forgot	tell / told	ring / rang	keep / kept	understand / understood
Row B	get / got	sell / sold	sing / sang	sleep / slept	stand / stood

C 🔄 Work with a partner. Follow the steps below to create sentences in a story.

1. Start at ❶.

2. Using only horizontal and vertical lines, connect the words to form a sentence. The words with punctuation end a sentence.

3. Write the sentence in the blanks below, changing the verbs from the present to the past tense.

4. Repeat with ❷, ❸, and so on.

5. Read the story aloud with your partner.

❶		❺ He	says	Hi	Teddy	how	are
	go	to	comes	over	to	me.	you?
❷ At	a	and	smiles	❹ He	don't	❻ I
the	party	at	his	name.	know	what
party	friend's	my	remember	don't	say.	to
I	house.	from	my	❸ I	❼ I	embarrassed!
see	a	student	old	school.	am	so

❶ ___I___ ___went___ ___to___ ___a___ ___party___ ___at___ ___my___ ___friend's___ ___house___.

❷ ___At___ ___the___ ___party___, _____ _____ _____ _____ _____ _____ _____

❸ _____ _____ _____ _____ _____

❹ _____ _____ _____ _____ _____ _____ _____

❺ _____ _____, " _____, _____, _____ _____ _____ "

❻ _____ _____ _____ _____ _____ _____

❼ _____ _____ _____ _____ _____

D  Use one of these ideas, or your own ideas, to tell a story. What did you do?

Tell a partner when you…

- left something important at home.
- forgot someone's name.
- couldn't remember an answer on a test.

6 COMMUNICATION

A What are some of your childhood memories? They can be happy, good, sad, or other memories. Make notes about your ideas in the chart.

A memory about...	Notes
my house or apartment.	
my parents.	
my brother(s) or sister(s).	
my grandparents.	
a favorite food.	
a friend.	
a toy.	
music.	
school.	
a vacation.	

B Get together with a partner. Take turns telling each other your memories.

> I have a happy memory about my old apartment. We lived on the second floor. Every day, I played with my best friend Lin.

C Discuss the questions with your partner.

1. Are any of your memories similar to your partner's?
2. Which memory is your favorite?

D Share your partner's favorite memory with the class.

Sleep helps you think and remember information better, studies show.
A 20-minute nap during the day can also improve your mood and memory.

1 VOCABULARY

A Review the meaning of the words in **blue** with your instructor.
Then circle a or b to complete the sentences about yourself.

1. I usually ＿＿ every night.
   a. **go to bed** at 10:00 or 11:00
   b. **stay up late** (midnight or later)

2. In bed, I ＿＿.
   a. **fall asleep** quickly
   b. **am awake** for a long time

3. I ＿＿ **wake up** at night.
   a. hardly ever
   b. often

4. In the morning, I usually ＿＿.
   a. **get up** (from bed) right away
   b. **stay in bed** for a while

Word Bank
Opposites
(be) asleep ↔ (be) awake
fall asleep ↔ wake up
go to bed ↔ stay up (late)
get up ↔ stay in bed

B 🗩 Tell a partner your answers in **A**. Your partner asks you one follow-up question.

> I usually stay up late every night.

> Really? When do you go to bed?

> At midnight.

C 👥 Are you and your partner similar or different? How? Tell another pair.

2 LISTENING

A  Look at the three sleep problems below. Do you know anyone with these problems? Tell a partner.

Some people…

- can't sleep.

- have *nightmares* (bad dreams).

- are *sleepwalkers*. (They wake up at night and do things, but they are asleep.)

> Sometimes my brother has nightmares.

B 🔊 **Listen for gist.** Listen to a news program about a woman named Mary. What is her problem? **CD 1 Track 42**

Mary _____.

a. has nightmares

b. is a sleepwalker

c. can't sleep

C 🔊  **Listen to sequence events.** Listen again. Put the events in order from 1 to 6. Then tell a partner Mary's story in your own words. **CD 1 Track 42**

_____ Mary went to bed at 10:00.

_____ She tried to buy ice cream.

_____ The police drove Mary home.

_____ She drove away.

_____ She got up later that night.

_____ The police woke her up.

Word Bank	
Present	**Past**
drive	drove
wake up	woke up

D  What caused Mary's problem? Choose a possible answer. Explain it to a partner.

Maybe Mary…

- was worried about something.

- was hungry.

- had a nightmare.

- my idea: _____.

3 READING

A 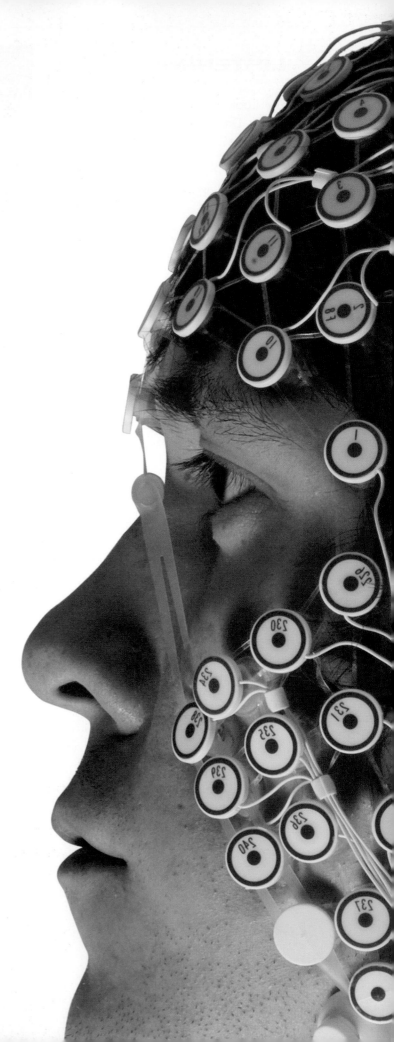 Discuss the questions in a small group. Then compare your answers with the class.

1. How many hours do you sleep each night?

2. What do you do when you can't sleep?

B **Identify the main idea.** Read the article. Then circle the correct answer to the question.

What is the main point of the article?

a. Today, people have healthier sleep patterns.

b. Waking up at night is not good for you.

c. It's normal to wake up at night.

d. Sleep research has a lot of problems.

C **Scan for details.** Read quickly to find answers to complete the chart.

Sleep Patterns	
People are in bed but are awake.	2 hours
People sleep.	
	1–3 hours
	4–5 hours

D Answer the questions with a partner.

1. What do you think of the sleep pattern described in the article? Is it healthy? Why or why not?

2. What would Dr. Wehr say: Are your sleep patterns healthy? Why or why not?

A STUDY OF SLEEP

It's 3:30 in the morning. Tomorrow is a busy day. You went to bed at 10:00. You need to get up at 6:00 in the morning. But you woke up in the middle of the night[1] and you can't fall asleep again! Why can't you sleep?

There may be a surprising answer. Dr. Thomas Wehr did some research on sleep. During the winter, he put people in a room with no artificial light (there was no light from lamps, TVs, or computers). Then, during the night, he studied the people's sleep patterns.[2]

What happened? The people went to bed, but they didn't fall asleep right away. Most were awake for two hours. Next, the people slept for four to five hours. Then they woke up, and they stayed awake and were active for one to three hours. Finally, the people slept again for four to five hours.

Dr. Wehr discovered a new sleep pattern. But maybe it's not new. In the past, before electric light, perhaps people slept this way. Nowadays, we sleep in a different way.

So, the next time you wake up in the middle of the night and can't sleep, relax! Your sleep patterns may be normal after all.

[1]If something happens *in the middle of the night*, it happens late at night, usually between 2:00 and 4:00 AM.

[2]A *pattern* is a repeated or regular way something happens.

4 GRAMMAR

A Turn to page 206. Complete the exercises. Then do **B–D** below.

The Simple Past Tense: *Yes / No* Questions				
Did	Subject	Verb		Short Answers
Did	you he they	stay up late wake up	last night?	Yes, I did. / No, I didn't. Yes, he did. / No, he didn't. Yes, they did. / No, they didn't.

The Simple Past Tense: *Wh-* Questions				
Wh- word	*did*	Subject	Verb	Answers
When	did	you she they	study?	(I / She / They studied) last night.
			get up?	(I / She / They got up) at 7:00.
What			happened to you?	I woke up late this morning.

B 🔗 Complete the conversation with past tense questions and answers using the words in parentheses. Then practice the conversation with a partner.

A: (1. you / go out) _Did you go out_ last night?

B: No, (2.) _____. I (3. stay) _____ home and (4. watch) _____ a movie.

A: Really? (5. what / you / watch) _____?

B: An old zombie movie called *28 Days Later*.

A: (6. you / like) _____ it?

B: Yes, (7.) _____, but later I (8. have) _____ nightmares.

A: (9. why / you / have) _____ nightmares?

B: Because it was a very scary movie! (10. what / you / do) _____ last night?

A: I (11. go) _____ to a party.

B: (12. who / you / go) _____ with?

A: Margo.

B: (13. you / have) _____ fun?

A: Yeah, we (14. have) _____ a great time at first. But then, something strange happened.

C 🔗 What strange thing happened to speaker A? Continue the conversation with your partner. Ask and answer four more past-tense questions to finish the story.

D 👥 Role-play your conversation for another pair. Whose story is the best?

5 WRITING

A Complete the paragraph with time words from the box.

finally	next	last	then	until

B  Read the paragraph and answer the questions with a partner.

1. When was the last time the writer stayed up late?
2. What did he do?
3. What time did he get up the next day?

C Answer the questions in **B** so they are true for you. Then use your notes and the words in **A** to write your own paragraph.

D Exchange your writing with a partner. Read his or her paragraph.

1. Are there any mistakes? If yes, circle them.
2. Answer the questions in **B** about your partner's writing.

> _____ Saturday, I stayed up late. I watched TV _____ 10:00, and *then* _____ I played video games _____ 12:30. I went to bed at 1:00, but I couldn't fall asleep! To relax, I listened to music and _____, I fell asleep at 3:00 AM. The _____ morning, I didn't get up _____ 11:00. I felt great, but my dad wasn't happy. He says I'm lazy!

6 COMMUNICATION

A Think about your sleep patterns for the last three days. Complete the chart.

	Yesterday	**The Day Before Yesterday**	**Three Days Ago**
Time I got up			
Time I went to bed			

B Use the words to write past tense *Yes / No* or *Wh-* questions.

1. what time / you / get up?
2. what time / you / go to bed?
3. you / fall asleep / right away?
4. you / wake up / during the night?
5. how many / hours / you / sleep?
6. what / you / dream / about?

> What time did you go to bed yesterday?
>
> I went to bed at 11.

C Ask a partner the questions in **B** about the last three days. Take notes.

D Read the sleep facts. Then answer the questions with a partner.

- Adults need seven to eight hours of sleep a night.
- It's best to go to bed and wake up at the same time each day.
- Light from computers and cell phones keeps you awake.

1. Do you and your partner have good sleep habits? Why or why not? Use your answers in **C** to explain.
2. What are two things you can do to sleep better?

E Share your answers in **D** with the class.

1 STORYBOARD

A Vivian and Jun are visiting a museum. Complete the conversation with a partner. Sometimes more than one answer is possible.

B Practice the conversation with a partner. Then switch roles and practice again.

2 SEE IT AND SAY IT

A 🔁 Look at the photos. Answer the questions about each place with a partner. Complete the sentence.

1. What season does this look like?

2. How's the weather?

3. What's the temperature?

4. In Punta Cana, it's _____, but in Harbin it's _____.

Punta Cana, Dominican Republic
85°F/29°C

Harbin, China
28°F/-2°C

B 🔁 Your partner is going on vacation to one of the places above. What should he or she pack? Use ideas in the box and one of your own. Explain your choices.

a camera	boots
a coat	sandals
a hat	shorts
a swimsuit	sunscreen
an umbrella	my idea: _____

Student A: You're going to Punta Cana.

Student B: You're going to Harbin.

> It's very cold there now, so I think you should pack a coat.

> Good idea. I will.

3 MEMORY GAME

A 🔗 Play a memory game with a partner. Read the instructions below.

Player A: Study the words and numbers in the chart below for 15 seconds. Then close your book and draw the chart on a piece of paper. Fill in as many words and numbers as you can remember.

Player B: Check Player A's answers.

cloudy	68
fall asleep	go sightseeing
whose	get up
529	admire
passport	musician

B 🔗 Play the game again. Switch roles. Use the chart below.

journalist	raining
explorer	memory
313	mine
should	wake up
47	unpack

C 🔗 Answer the questions with a partner.

1. How many words did you remember?
2. Which words did you forget?
3. Which words were easy to remember? Why?

D Choose four words from each chart and write sentences using them. At least two sentences should be in the past tense.

E 🔗 Tell a partner your sentences. Then your partner asks you one question about each sentence.

Yesterday, I fell asleep early.

When did you go to bed?

4 LISTEN: QUESTIONS AND ANSWERS

A 🔊 You will hear a question and then four answers about each photo. Circle the letter that best answers the question. **CD 1 Track 44**

1.

              A   B   C   D

2.

              A   B   C   D

3.

              A   B   C   D

5 SPEAK FOR A MINUTE!

A Read the questions and think about your answers.

1. What's your favorite season? Why? What's the weather like?

2. Where did you go on your last vacation? How did you prepare for the trip?

3. Describe your early years (from birth to age five).

4. What are two interesting jobs?

> I was born in...

5. Who do you admire?

6. Talk about a time when you forgot something. What happened?

B 👥 Get into a group of three.

1. Take turns. Choose a question from **A**.

2. Answer the question by talking for one minute without stopping and you get one point.

3. Continue until there are no more questions.

4. The winner is the person with the most points.

7 CITY LIFE

Traffic speeds by on a busy night in Shanghai, China.

Look at the photo. Answer the questions.

1 What city is this? Do you know anything about this city?

2 Is your city a good place to live? Why or why not?

3 What do you like most about your city? What do you dislike?

UNIT GOALS

1 Identify places in a neighborhood

2 Ask for and give directions

3 Give your location

4 Explain why a city is or isn't a good place to live

The Stockholm Metro is famous for its art.

1 VIDEO My City: Stockholm

A ▶ Read the list below. Then watch the video with the sound off. Check (✓) the things Stockholm has.

Word Bank
diverse = different
exhibition = a public art event

Stockholm has _____.

☑ beautiful old buildings

☑ a river

☑ nice parks with trees and flowers

☐ a lot of very large cars

☑ many immigrants (people from other countries)

☑ some noise from nearby factories

☐ a beautiful subway

☑ many well-dressed people

B ▶ Watch the video. Match the phrases to form sentences from the video. One phrase is extra.

1. Stockholm is known for its long summer days _b_
2. The people here are as diverse _d_
3. It's part of the lifestyle to _a_
4. The Stockholm Metro has the world's longest art exhibition. _c_

a. look good and dress nice.

b. and the never-ending, icy winter nights.

c. It's 110 kilometers.

d. as the fruits and flowers on sale.

e. stay up late at night.

C 🔁 Answer the questions with a partner.

1. What is something you learned about Stockholm? Do you want to visit this city?
2. Does your city have any of the things in **A**?
3. My city is known for _____.

2 VOCABULARY

A Look at this list of places found in a **neighborhood** (the area around your home). Which words do you know? Do you know any other words that end in *club*, *salon*, *shop*, *stand*, *station*, or *store*?

health club	**coffee shop**	**train station**
hair salon	**newsstand**	**grocery store**

Word Bank
health club = **gym**
coffee shop = **cafe**
newsstand = **kiosk**
grocery store = **supermarket**
ATM = **cash machine**

B 🔁 Complete the location names below by using the words in the box. Then look at the photos and label the places. Compare your answers with a partner's.

1. ATM	5. department _Shop_	9. police _Station_
2. book _Store_	6. gas _Station_	10. taxi _Station_
3. bus _Station_	7. nail _Salon_	
4. copy _____	8. night _Club_	

club	station
stand	shop
salon	store

C 🔁 What do you do at the places in **A** and **B**? Which places do you visit often? Discuss with a partner.

> I go to the train station every morning. I take the train to school.

The train station in Lubeck, Germany

3 LISTENING

A 🔊 **Pronunciation: Stress in compound noun phrases.** Listen and repeat.
What do you notice about the stress pattern of these nouns? **CD 2 Track 2**

1. health club   4. taxi stand
2. coffee shop   5. copy shop
3. train station   6. nail salon

B 🔊 **Listen for details.** Read the sentences. Then listen to Pablo and Yuki's conversation.
Circle T for *true* or F for *false*. **CD 2 Track 3**

1.	It's Pablo's neighborhood.	(T)	F
2.	Yuki lives nearby.	T	(F)
3.	Yuki has a lot of homework.	(T)	F
4.	The library opens at noon.	T	(F)
5.	Yuki wants to buy a book.	(T)	F
6.	The bookstore has a cafe.	(T)	F

C 🔊 **Make and check predictions.** Look at the chart. Can you guess the answers? Listen
again and complete the chart with other ways of saying these ideas. **CD 2 Track 3**

Original idea	What you hear
1. How are you?	_How is is_ going?
2. Is this your neighborhood?	_do_ you _live_ around here?
3. Where are you going?	Where are you _going_?
4. drink a cup of coffee	_want have_ a cup of coffee
5. Don't talk (to me).	No _____ allowed.

D 🔄 Where is the most popular place to hang out in your neighborhood? Describe it to a partner.

Do you live near a train line or bus route?
When does the first and last train or bus
run? How many stations or stops are there?
Share your information with your class.

4 SPEAKING

A 🔊 Min Chul and Jan are driving to the movies. Look at the map and listen to their conversation. What are they looking for? Where is it? **CD 2 Track 4**

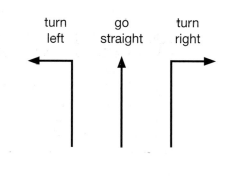

MIN CHUL: Uh-oh. I think we're running out of gas.

JAN: OK... where's the nearest gas station?

MIN CHUL: I don't know. Let's ask someone.

JAN: Excuse me.

MAN: Yes?

JAN: Is there a gas station near here?

MAN: Yes. Go straight and turn right on Court Street. Go one block. It's on the corner of Court Street and First Avenue.

JAN: Thanks!

B 👥 Practice the conversation in groups of three.

SPEAKING STRATEGY

Useful Expressions	
Asking for and giving directions	
Asking about a place in general	Excuse me. Is there a (gas station) near here? Yes. Go one block. There's one on the corner of (Court Street and First Avenue).
Asking about a specific place	Excuse me. Where's the (Bridge Theater)? It's on (Jay Street). Go straight and turn right (on Jay Street). It's in the middle of the block.
Speaking tip	
To start asking for directions, you can ask, *Are you familiar with this neighborhood / area?*	

turn left ←   go straight ↑   turn right →

C 🔄 Take turns asking a partner for directions to different places. Start at the **X**. Use the Useful Expressions to help you.

D 🔄 With a partner, choose one place on the map and make a short conversation. Use the conversation at the top of the page as a model. Perform it for the class.

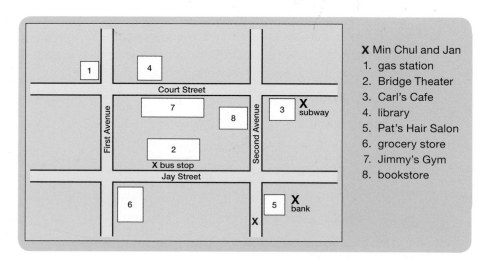

X Min Chul and Jan
1. gas station
2. Bridge Theater
3. Carl's Cafe
4. library
5. Pat's Hair Salon
6. grocery store
7. Jimmy's Gym
8. bookstore

5 GRAMMAR

A Turn to page 207. Complete the exercises. Then do **B–D** below.

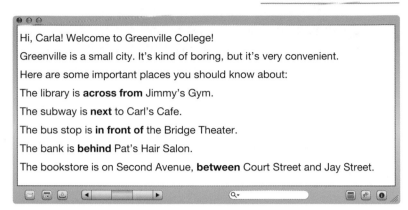

at 2:00
on Spear Street
at 226 Spear Street
on the second floor

B Carla is a new student at Greenville College. Read the email to Carla. As you read, notice the **bold** words.

1. Underline the places mentioned in the email.

2. Work with a partner. Use the map on page 99 to find the places mentioned in the email.

> Hi, Carla! Welcome to Greenville College!
>
> Greenville is a small city. It's kind of boring, but it's very convenient.
>
> Here are some important places you should know about:
>
> The library is **across from** Jimmy's Gym.
>
> The subway is **next** to Carl's Cafe.
>
> The bus stop is **in front of** the Bridge Theater.
>
> The bank is **behind** Pat's Hair Salon.
>
> The bookstore is on Second Avenue, **between** Court Street and Jay Street.

C Look at the street scene below and answer the questions.

1. What's in front of the Mexican restaurant?

   Bus stop is in the front of the Mexican restaurant.

2. What's across from the theater?

   People across from the theater.

3. What's behind the cafe?

   Nail salon is behind the cafe.

4. What's next to the theater?

   Mexican food is next to the theater.

5. What's in front of the gym?

   Newsstand is in front of the gym.

6. What's between the gym and the bank?

   Cafe is between the gym and the bank.

D Practice the conversation below with a partner. Then make a plan to meet at one of the places in **C** (or choose your own place). Create a new conversation. Use the conversation as a model.

A: Where are you now?

B: I'm going to the supermarket. Why don't you join me? We can shop together.

A: OK. Where's the supermarket exactly?

B: It's at 226 Spear Street.

A: Oh, I remember. It's next to the department store, right?

B: That's right. Let's meet at 2:00.

A: OK. See you then.

6 COMMUNICATION

A 🔧 Read the information. Then answer the questions with a partner.

Ms. Smith and Ms. Jones live in the same apartment building at 50 Dean Street. They have tea together every Thursday afternoon at 4:00.

On this Thursday, Ms. Smith doesn't answer the doorbell. Ms. Jones calls Mr. Busby, the apartment manager. He has a key to Ms. Smith's apartment. He opens the door and sees Ms. Smith on the floor. She is dead!

Later, the police find an apartment key under Ms. Smith's sofa. The number on the key is 300. The key belongs to the killer.

1. Who are Ms. Smith and Ms. Jones?
2. Who is Mr. Busby?
3. What does Mr. Busby see?
4. What do the police find? Why is it important?

The neighbors at 50 Dean Street

Ms. Smith   Ms. Jones   Mr. and Mrs. Busby

Ms. Sanchez   Mr. Hu   Dr. Lewis

B 🔧 Work with your partner to find the killer. Try to be the first in the class.

Partner A: Read the sentences to your partner.

Partner B: Write the names and room numbers on the doors.

Ms. Smith lives in apartment 305.

Mr. and Mrs. Busby live across from Ms. Smith.

Ms. Sanchez lives between Dr. Lewis and Mr. and Mrs. Busby.

Mr. Hu lives across from Ms. Sanchez.

The apartment next to Ms. Smith's is 303.

Mr. Hu lives next to Miss Jones.

Ms. Jones lives across from apartment 300.

> Let's see. Ms. Smith lives in apartment 305.

> Ms. Smith... 305... OK, got it.

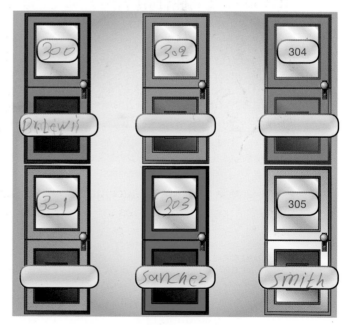

Cities with the world's worst traffic:
1. _____
2. Istanbul, Turkey
3. Mexico City, Mexico

Traffic in Istanbul, Turkey

1 VOCABULARY

A   Guess: Which city has the worst traffic? Check your answer at the bottom-right of the page.

B   Read the information. Then take turns asking and answering the questions below with a partner.

The problem with traffic:	What can cities do?
• During **rush hour** (the busy times in the morning and evening), people are often **stuck in traffic**. Their cars don't move. In **heavy traffic**, a 30-minute trip is often an hour. • Having many cars on the road causes a lot of air **pollution**. Worldwide, air pollution kills over three million people every year.*	• At the moment, Jakarta, Istanbul, and Mexico City all have large **populations** of nine million people or more. But these cities don't have enough **public transportation** (buses, subways, and trains). Each city is trying to build more.

*Source: The World Health Organization

1. When are people usually stuck in traffic?

2. In heavy traffic, how long is a 30-minute trip?

3. What causes air pollution?

4. What are the three cities above trying to do about traffic?

5. In your city, how is…

the traffic during rush hour?	heavy	so-so	light
the air?	very polluted	so-so	not very polluted
public transportation?	terrible	so-so	excellent

> The traffic during rush hour is very heavy in Tokyo.

Word Bank

Opposites

a lot of ↔ a little (pollution) (*n.*)

very ↔ not very (polluted) (*adj.*)

heavy ↔ light (traffic)

A. 1. Jakarta, Indonesia

2 LISTENING

A 🔲 Answer the questions with a partner.

1. Look at the map. In what country is the state of Vermont?

2. Look at the photos. What things do you see?

B 🔊 **Listen for context.** Listen. Circle the correct answer to complete the sentence. **CD 2 Track 5**

You are listening to _____.

a. a news report   c. an interview

b. an advertisement   d. a class lecture

C 🔊 **Listen for details.** Read the sentences. Then listen again and circle the correct words. **CD 2 Track 5**

1. The state of Vermont is very polluted / not polluted at all.

2. Its capital city has a small / large population.

3. During rush hour in Vermont's capital city, most people are / aren't stuck in traffic.

4. Vermont is famous for its sweet maple syrup / ice cream.

5. Outside the capital city, there are a lot of things to do outdoors / indoors.

D 🔲 Answer the questions with a partner.

1. Do you want to visit Vermont? Why or why not?

2. Is there an area in your country like Vermont? What is its population? What is it famous for? Do you like this place?

3 READING

A  **Make predictions.** Look at the title, introduction, and photos. What do you think are some of the pros (good things) and cons (bad things) of living in these two cities? Tell your partner.

B **Read for details.** Work with a partner. Copy the chart into your notebook. Then:

Student A: Read about Lima.

Student B: Read about Hong Kong.

What does the reading say about your city? Complete the chart. Write *NG* if the information is not given.

	Lima	Hong Kong
weather		
public transportation		
traffic		
food		
neighborhoods		
pollution		
housing		
things to do outside the city		

C Tell your partner about your city in **B**. Your partner listens and takes notes.

D Choose a fact that is not given (NG) in the chart in **B**. Go online and find information about the topic. Add it to the chart.

E Answer the questions with a partner. Use information in the chart to explain.

1. Do you prefer Lima or Hong Kong? Why?

2. Compare your city to Lima or Hong Kong in three ways. How is your city the same or different?

> There's heavy traffic in our city center, too.

CITY LIVING

What are the pros and cons of living in different cities around the world? Today we focus on Lima and Hong Kong.

Plaza San Martin, Lima

Victoria Harbor, Hong Kong

When people think of Peru, they imagine rain forests, mountains, and Machu Picchu. These things are not in Lima, but this city is still a nice place to live and visit for several reasons. For one thing, many other cities in Latin America have hot, humid weather in the summers. But Lima doesn't. It has pleasant[1] weather all year (15° C / 59° F to 27° C / 81° F). Many of the city's older neighborhoods are beautiful and have small hotels, museums, clubs, and cafes. The Historic Center has some of the world's best colonial architecture, and there are even pre-Incan ruins.[2]

If you want to spend some time outside the city, it is easy to visit beaches, rain forests, and mountains near Lima. The city also has a lot of public transportation, but there's heavy traffic in the city center, especially during rush hour. Be careful walking or driving there!

Hong Kong—once a small fishing village— is an international business center and an interesting mix of East and West, old and new. Modern buildings are next to small temples. Popular nightclubs are close to traditional teahouses. Busy crowds fill the streets at all hours of the day, but outside the city, there are parks for walking or relaxing. Hong Kong is also famous for its delicious street food and its many excellent restaurants with food from all over Asia, Europe, and the Americas.

There are many great things about Hong Kong, but there are some problems, too. Housing isn't cheap. With a population of over seven million, it is one of the world's most expensive cities to live in. Also, the pollution in Hong Kong is not bad, but in the summer and winter, the air is sometimes polluted.

[1] If the weather is *pleasant*, it is comfortable, not too hot or too cold.
[2] *Ruins* are the parts of an old building that are still standing. The *Inca* people had a very large empire; its center was in Peru.

4 GRAMMAR

A Turn to page 208. Complete the exercises. Then do **B–D** below.

Questions and Answers with *How much / How many*		
	Count nouns	**Noncount nouns**
	How many parks are there in your city?	**How much** pollution is there?

Affirmative	(There are) **a lot / many.**
	          some / a few.
	          two.
		(There's) **a lot.**
		          some / a little.

Negative	There are**n't many. / Not many.** There are**n't any. / None.**	There is**n't much. / Not much.** There is**n't any. / None.**

B Complete the questions with *much* or *many.* Then think about your answers to the questions.

In your city…

1. how ___many___ people are there?
2. how ___much___ smog is there in the air today?
3. how ___many___ parks are there?
4. how ___many___ taxis are there?
5. how ___much___ noise is there?
6. how ___many___ crime is there?
7. how ___much___ fun things to do at night are there?
8. how ___much___ very cold days are there?
9. how ___much___ hot days are there?
10. how ___many___ traffic is there?

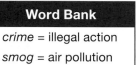

C  Ask and answer the questions in **B** with a partner. Use the words in **bold** in the chart in your answer.

> How many parks are there in your city?

> Not many. Maybe two.

Lumpini Park, Bangkok, Thailand

D In your opinion, is your city a good place to live? Why or why not? Use your answers in **C** to explain to a partner.

> There aren't many parks in this city. We need more parks so people can relax and exercise.

5 WRITING

A Read the brochure. This city wants to host the 2032 Summer Olympics. In your opinion, is it a good city?

B 🔄 Imagine that your city wants to host the 2032 Summer Olympics. Make your own brochure with a partner.

1. Include this information about your city in your brochure:
   - the weather
   - public transportation
   - hotels and restaurants
   - airports and train stations
   - traffic
   - the amount of pollution
   - nightlife (clubs, theaters, concerts)
   - our idea: _____

2. Think about how to organize the brochure.
   - How will you present the information?
   - What pictures will you use?

Remember to be positive! The class will choose the best brochure to represent your city.

PLEASANT VALLEY
wants to host the 2032 Summer Olympics!

Pleasant Valley has over 300 days of sun a year!

There are many great neighborhoods in **Pleasant Valley**.

The Downtown Area is the center of business and nightlife. Public transportation is excellent. There is a subway system. It connects to an international airport. There are also a lot of buses and cabs. It's easy to go everywhere.

The Northern District is famous for its hotels and restaurants.

South Beach has 20 kilometers of unpolluted beaches and a new sports stadium.

6 COMMUNICATION

A 👥 Present your brochures.

- **The presenters:** With your partner, present your brochure to the class. Each person should explain a part of the brochure.

- **The listeners:** For each presentation, complete these sentences on a piece of paper:

I liked _____ about this brochure.

I wanted to know more about _____.

> I wanted to know more about the weather in summer. That's important for visitors.

B 🔄 Look at your notes in **A**. Which brochure and presentation was the best? Why? Tell a partner.

C 👥 As a class, choose the best brochure.

8 ALL ABOUT YOU

Look at the photo. Answer the questions.

1 What are the people doing?

2 Can you do what they are doing?

3 What sports do you like to do?

UNIT GOALS

1 Talk about sports that you like and do

2 Invite and offer using *Do you want*

3 Describe different personalities

4 Talk about how often you do things

Photographers take photos of a surfer in Oahu, Hawaii, in the United States.

A group of children do yoga outside.

1 **VIDEO** Yoga in Schools

A Look at the picture. Have you seen people do this before? Does it look fun? Tell a partner.

B You are going to watch a video about teaching yoga in school. Read the sentences. What do people say about yoga? Fill in the missing words.

1. "Sometimes it takes a lot of courage to just be a little bit more still and not _____."

2. "I forget about the _____ things that are happening."

3. "I feel _____ and calm."

4. "Before, I'm always just running around and not really paying attention, but after yoga, I feel, like _____ and can do my work faster."

5. "Yoga is simply a _____..."

6. "_____% of our students say that after yoga class, they are more ready to learn."

C Look at your answers in **B**. Did the students enjoy their yoga class? Explain your answer to a partner.

D Is having a yoga class in your school a good idea? Why or why not? Tell your partner.

2 VOCABULARY

A 🔁 The sports words in each column are missing the same vowel (*a, e, i, o,* or *u*). Fill in the missing letters. Work with a partner. Which words go with *play* or *do*? with *go*?

1. b**a**seb**a**ll

2. b**a**sketb**a**ll

3. volleyb**a**ll

4. b**a**dminton

5. sw**i**mm**i**ng

6. p**i**ng pong

7. surf**i**ng

8. sk**i**ing

9. y**o**ga

10. jud**o**

11. b**o**wling

12. j**u**gging

13. hock**e**y

14. t**e**nnis

15. socc**e**r

16. pilat**e**s

B 🔁 Ask a partner these questions.

1. Can you play _____ well?

2. Name one person who does _____. Why are they good at it?

3. When was the last time you went _____? How was it?

> Can you play volleyball well?

> No, I can't. I'm too short!

> ℹ️ **play / do** + noun
> You **play** a game of *soccer, basketball,* etc.
> Also with **play:** *cards, darts, golf, rugby*
> You **do** martial arts (*judo, kickboxing,* etc.) and other activities. Also with **do:** *gymnastics, crafts, puzzles*
>
> **go** + noun + *-ing*
> You can often do activities with **go** alone. Also with **go:** *camping, climbing, fishing, golfing*

3 LISTENING

A **Use visual cues.** Look at the title in **B** and the photo at the bottom of the page. What is this listening about?

B 🔊 🔁 **Make predictions.** Read the paragraph. Then listen and complete it. Answer the question below. **CD 2 Track 7**

From Physician to Beach Bum

In the 1950s, Dorian "Doc" Paskowitz was a successful physician. He was handsome and in good health. To many people, Doc's life seemed perfect. But it wasn't. Doc was _____. He didn't like his work. The one thing he loved was _____. So one day, Doc decided to change his life. He decided to follow his _____.

What do you think happened to Doc Paskowitz and his family? Circle your answer(s). Then explain your ideas to a partner.

a. He surfed all the time.

c. He traveled with his family.

b. He became a doctor in another city.

d. He built a house on the beach.

C 🔊 **Listen for gist.** Listen to more of the story and complete the sentences. **CD 2 Track 8**

1. Doc and his wife had _____. 2. The family became a _____.

D 🔊 **Listen for details.** Listen to the rest of the story and choose the correct answer for each item. **CD 2 Track 9**

1. They lived _____.

   a. in a small camper   b. a busy life

2. They visited places like _____.

   a. California and Australia   b. Mexico and Venezuela

3. The family had _____.

   a. a lot of money   b. a small business

4. The children did not _____.

   a. go to school   b. learn to surf well

E 🔁 What do you think of the Paskowitz family? Did they have a good life? Why or why not? Discuss with a partner.

WORLD LINK

Where are the best places in the world to go surfing? Research three locations online and report back to your class.

4 SPEAKING

A 🔊 Listen to the conversation. Underline Connie's offer. Circle Gina's invitation. **CD 2 Track 10**

CONNIE: Hey, Gina. Do you want some ice cream?

GINA: No, thanks. I'm going out.

CONNIE: Really? Where are you going?

GINA: I'm going to play tennis. Do you want to come?

CONNIE: Sorry, I can't. I need to study.

GINA: Well, come later then. We're playing all afternoon.

CONNIE: It sounds nice... but I'm not very good at tennis.

GINA: Don't worry about that. You don't have to play. You can just watch. Come on, it'll be fun.

CONNIE: Well, OK. I'll see you in an hour.

GINA: OK, see you later... and maybe we can have some ice cream afterwards!

B 🗩 Practice the conversation with a partner.

SPEAKING STRATEGY

C Complete the information below.

1. Sport or activity I like to do: _____

2. Place to do it: _____

3. Day / time to do it: _____

D 🗩 Make a conversation with a partner. Use the conversation above and the Useful Expressions to help you. Follow the steps below.

1. Invite your partner to do your activity.

2. Your partner should first decline the invitation.

3. Next, your partner accepts it.

4. Switch roles and repeat.

E 🗩 Perform one of your conversations for the class.

Useful Expressions	
Inviting and offering with _Do you want_	
Inviting	Do you want to come? [_want_ + _to_ + verb] Sure, I'd love to! Sorry, I can't. I'm busy. Um, no thanks. I'm not good at...
Offering	Do you want some ice cream? [_want_ + noun] Yes, please. / Yes, thanks. No, thank you. / No, thanks. I'm fine.
Speaking tip	
You can also use _would like_ to invite: _Would you like to come with us?_	

5 GRAMMAR

A Turn to page 209. Complete the exercise. Then do **B–D** below.

Verb + Infinitive	Verb + Noun
I **love** / **like** <u>to play</u> volleyball.	I **love** / **like** <u>sports</u>.
I **forgot** <u>to explain</u> the rules.	I **need** my <u>uniform</u>.
Verbs like *forget, hate, learn, like, love, need, decide, plan, prepare,* and *want* can be followed by a noun or the infinitive (*to* + the base form of the verb).	

B 🔊 **Pronunciation: Reduced *to.*** Listen and repeat. What do you notice about the pronunciation of the word *to* in each sentence? **CD 2 Track 11**

1. I like to play golf.
2. She likes to go jogging.
3. I love to sleep late.
4. He hates to study.
5. We plan to fly to Paris.
6. Do you like to play chess?
7. I want to be early.
8. I hate to be late.

C This is Jenna. For each picture, make up a sentence about her or the people she's with. Use the verbs given.

want

SKI LESSONS

learn

love

ROCK

not enjoy

decide

CHEAP TICKETS!

TAKE A VACATION

Let's go together!

prefer

D 🔁 Ask and answer the questions with a partner.

What is one thing…

    you love to do on the weekend?

    you need to study harder?

    you want to do by the end of the year?

What are two things…

    you plan to do soon?

    you want for your next birthday?

    you like about your school?

> What are two things you like about your school?

> Let's see… I like my classmates. They're friendly. And I also like…

6 COMMUNICATION

A Read the questions below. Write your answers under *My answer* in the chart.

	My answer	Classmate's name	Classmate's answer
		Lubna	Amina
1. What's your favorite sport or event to watch?	concert	twnss	soccer
2. Which sport do you most like to play?	Saccer	Tenss	Swiming
3. Who's your favorite athlete?	Ronaldo		Mohammed Salah
4. What do you want for your birthday?	car	gold	iphon 13
5. What movie do you want to see?	funy movg	love movg	Acshin
6. What is one thing you learned in the last year?	don't trest eap	stong	Driving
7. Where do you plan to go next year?	French	Magame	Moldif
0. What do you want to do this weekend?	Park	Mall	Pous

B 🔄 For each question, interview a *different* classmate. Write each person's name and answer in the chart.

C 🔵 Get into a group of three. For each question, read a classmate's answer. Do *not* say the person's name. Your group guesses which classmate gave that answer.

> I asked the question, "What's your favorite sport or event to watch?" This person loves to watch soccer.

> I know! That's Mateo.

> Yes, that's right!

Penny and Pearl are both friendly. They are also **bright** (intelligent). However, their friends say they are very different.

Penny

Pearl

Penny is very **organized**. She knows where everything is in her apartment.

Penny is really **ambitious**. Someday, she wants to have her own company.

Penny's very **careful** with her money. In fact, she's a little bit **selfish**—sometimes she doesn't like to share.

Penny is somewhat **reserved**. She has two or three close friends and doesn't go out a lot.

Pearl's apartment is kind of **messy**: there are dirty dishes in the sink and magazines on the floor.

Pearl is very **laid-back** (relaxed) about life and work.

Sometimes Pearl is **careless** with money—she forgets to pay her bills.

But she's very **generous**. She will share anything with you.

Pearl is **talkative**. She talks to everyone and is comfortable at parties.

1 VOCABULARY

> **i** You can use these words to make adjectives stronger:
> **very** organized   **really** ambitious
> You can use these words to weaken negative adjectives:
> **a little (bit)** selfish   **somewhat** reserved   **kind of** messy

A Penny and Pearl are cousins. Read about their personalities. Then answer the questions with a partner.

1. Which words in **blue** are opposites?

2. Which words do you think are positive? Which are negative?

B Look at the pictures. Which items belong to Pearl? to Penny? How do you know? Write their names.

1. _____   2. _____   3. _____   4. _____

C  Which words in blue do you think describe Penny? Which describe Pearl? Explain your answers to a partner.

A **competitive** person wants to be more successful than other people.

An **impulsive** person does things suddenly without thinking carefully.

A **creative** person has a lot of new ideas, especially in the arts (music, dance, etc.).

A **private** person doesn't like others to know how he or she feels.

D Is your personality more like Pearl's or Penny's? How? Tell a partner.

2 LISTENING

A Use visual cues. Look at the photos. What are the people doing? Guess: How do the people feel?

B Infer; Listen for gist. A man is going to talk about two personality types: Type A and Type B. Listen and circle the correct answer. **CD 2 Track 12**

1. The talk is happening at a company / hospital / school.

2. Photo 1 / Photo 2 / Both photos above show(s) a Type A person.

C Listen for details. Look up any unfamiliar words below. Then listen again. Which words describe a Type A person? Check (✓) them. **CD 2 Track 12**

☐ angry   ☐ laid-back   ☐ patient

☐ competitive   ☐ nervous   ☐ a workaholic

D Answer the questions with a partner.

1. Guess: What words describe a Type B person? Make a list of your ideas.

2. Are you more Type A or Type B? Why?

3. "Being Type A can be bad for your health." Do you agree or disagree with this sentence? Why?

3 READING

A **Use background knowledge.** Look at the title of the reading and the four personality types. Do you know about any of the people in the photos? What do they do?

B **Make predictions.** Guess the answers about the four personality types. Sometimes more than one answer is possible.

This person...	The Dreamer	The Partner	The Thinker	The Artist
1. likes to follow rules.		✓		
2. is creative.				
3. listens to others' opinions.				
4. is a problem solver.				
5. has strong ideas about things.				
6. is careful.				
7. is organized and helpful.				
8. doesn't like change.				
9. does things without thinking carefully.				

C **Scan for information.** Look quickly at the reading to find the answers in **B**. Correct any incorrect answers.

D 🔄 **Read for details.** Read the passage again. Which one or two of the personality types describe(s) you? your best friend? your parents? Why? Tell a partner.

> I'm a mix of the Dreamer and the Artist.

WORLD LINK

Research one of the people talked about in the reading.

Does the personality type describe him or her? Why or why not?

LIFE STYLE

Malala Yousafzai

The Dreamer

A Dreamer thinks there is a "right" way to do things. This person wants to live in the "perfect world." A Dreamer is often hardworking, organized, and very passionate[1] about his or her work. Many are good listeners and want to help others. Many Dreamers work as activists, lawyers, and in leadership roles.

[1] If you are *passionate* about something, you care about it a lot.

The Partner

A Partner wants to be in a group. For this person, rules and group harmony are important. Tradition is, too. Partners are often reserved, careful people, and change makes them nervous. Many do well as managers, police officers, and politicians.

Famous Partners: Queen Elizabeth II, UN Secretary-General Ban Ki-Moon

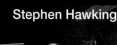

Ban Ki-Moon

The Thinker

For Thinkers, understanding things is very important. They like to solve problems and make new things. Thinkers can also be competitive. They like to win. They are careful, ambitious people and often have very strong opinions. Many Thinkers work as scientists, inventors, politicians, and engineers.

Famous Thinkers: filmmaker and inventor James Cameron, scientist Stephen Hawking, businesswoman Sheryl Sandberg

Stephen Hawking

The Artist

Artists want to be free. They don't want to follow the rules all the time. Artists like action and are often impulsive. They also like trying new things, and they aren't afraid of change. Like Thinkers, many Artists have strong opinions. They do well in creative fields like music, acting, design, and in some sports.

Famous Artists: fashion designer Yang Li, soccer player Luis Suárez, singer Beyoncé

Beyoncé

Famous Dreamers: activist Malala Yousafzai, lawyer Amal Ramzi Clooney, journalist and food activist Carlo Petrini

4 GRAMMAR

A Turn to page 209. Complete the exercises. Then do **B** and **C** below.

How often...? Frequency Expressions			
How often do you see your best friend?	(I see her)	**every**	day / Monday / week / month / summer.
		once **twice** **three times** **several times**	a day / a week / a month / a year.
		all the time. **once in a while**.	
	Hardly ever.		

B Answer the questions about yourself.

How often do you...   Answer

1. go shopping and spend too much money?   I spend too much money once in a while _____.

2. watch TV? _____.

3. buy things for your friends or family? _____.

4. play video games and win? _____.

5. go on dates? _____.

6. text your friends? _____.

7. clean your desk? _____.

8. stay up late studying or working? _____.

C 🗨 Take turns asking and answering the questions in **B** with a partner.
Are you similar or different?

> I play games and win all the time. I'm really competitive.

> I only clean my desk once in a while. I'm kind of messy.

5 WRITING

A Read the student's personality profile. What adjectives does he use to describe himself? Circle them.

What are you like?

Usually, I'm kind of shy. For example, I like to go to parties, but it's hard to talk to new people. I feel nervous, so I'm kind of quiet. But once you get to know me, I'm really talkative. I like to tell jokes, and I'm very funny. I'm also a little competitive. I play video games with my friends all the time, and I hate to lose. For this reason, they hardly ever win!

B Think of three personality adjectives to describe yourself. Write them below. Also use one of the words given with the adjective.

I'm very / kind of / a little _____.

I'm very / kind of / a little _____.

I'm very / kind of / a little _____.

C Write about yourself. Remember to explain each idea in **B** with an example.

D Exchange your paper with a partner. Circle any mistakes. Then answer the question in **A** about your partner. Did you learn anything new about him or her? Tell the class.

6 COMMUNICATION

A Use the chart to interview a partner. Circle his or her answers.

Personality Quiz

Questions	Answers	
How often do you clean your room?	**a.** once a week	**b.** once in a while
How often do friends ask for your advice?	**a.** all the time	**b.** hardly ever
What is more important?	**a.** being kind	**b.** being honest
What is more important?	**a.** agreeing with the group	**b.** saying my opinion
Are you careful with money?	**a.** Yes, most of the time.	**b.** No, not really.
What is more important to you?	**a.** success	**b.** happiness
You're playing a game. Which sentence describes you?	**a.** I'm very competitive. I hate to lose.	**b.** I'm kind of laid-back. I want to win, but if I lose, it's OK.
Your cell phone isn't working. What do you do?	**a.** try to fix it myself	**b.** ask for help
What is more important?	**a.** facts	**b.** feelings
What do you want in your life?	**a.** many different experiences	**b.** the same job
What is more important?	**a.** being free	**b.** being careful
You get a free ticket to Paris. The plane leaves tomorrow. Do you go?	**a.** Yes! I'm very impulsive.	**b.** No way! That's too scary.

B Total your partner's points for each color (a = 2 points, b = 1 point). Read about the color(s) with the *most* points on page 218 and tell your partner about his or her personality type(s).

C Do you agree with your description? Explain your opinion to your partner.

9CHANGE

People do yoga at the Red Rocks
Amphitheatre, Colorado, US.

Look at the photo. Answer the questions.

1 Where are these people?

2 What are they doing?

3 Why do you think they're doing this?

UNIT GOALS

1 Talk about changes in your life

2 Describe future goals

3 Make and respond to requests

4 Talk about future plans and goals

1 VIDEO Keep Clean in 2015

A  Do you do any chores? Which ones? Can you think of ways to make them easier to do? Tell a partner.

B ▶ Watch the video. Put the advice in the correct order.

_____5_____ Make a schedule.

_____3_____ Always make progress.

_____1_____ Set realistic goals.

_____2_____ Stay focused.

_____4_____ Reward yourself.

C Can you think of any other advice for making changes like this? Tell a partner.

2 VOCABULARY

A  Look at the two pictures of Martin. How are they different? Tell your partner one or two differences.

> In the first picture, Martin is working at home. In the second...

last year

this year

B Look at the picture of Martin this year. His life has changed a lot. Which sentences describe his changes? Circle the correct sentence.

1. Martin **lost his job**. / Martin **found a new job**.

2. He's **making** more **money**. / He's **making** less **money**.

3. He **lost weight**. / He **gained weight**.

4. He exercises a lot now. He's **in good shape**. / He's **in bad shape**.

5. He **started** smoking. / He **stopped** smoking.

C  What do you want to do this year? Circle your answer(s). Tell a partner.

get in shape   earn more money

find a new job   start / quit _____

other idea: _I want to focus on College_

Word Bank

found a new job = **got a new job**

making more money = **earning more money**

in bad shape = **out of shape**

stopped smoking = **quit smoking**

> **i** The words *stop, quit,* and *start* are often followed by a word ending in *-ing*:
> He **stopped** *smoking* and **started** *exercising*.
> Please **quit** *talking* and **start** *working*.

3 LISTENING

A 🔊 **Pronunciation: Contrastive stress.** Read the sentences. Then listen and repeat. **CD 2 Track 14**

1. She <u>got</u> a new job. She's really happy about it.

2. You're in really <u>good</u> shape! How often do you work out?

3. He <u>stopped</u> smoking. That's great!

B 🔊 💬 **Pronunciation: Contrastive stress.** Now listen to three dialogs. Underline the new information that is stressed in each response. Then practice the dialogs with a partner. **CD 2 Track 15**

Many cultures celebrate the New Year as a time to start over. The celebration in Brazil includes fireworks.

A: Is she making more money in her new job?
B: No, she's making <u>less</u> money.

A: How's your diet going? Did you lose weight or gain weight?
B: Unfortunately, I <u>gained</u> two kilos.

A: I heard that you quit drinking soda recently.
B: No, actually, I quit drinking <u>coffee</u>.

C 💬 Many people make changes, or resolutions, at the New Year. What is one change you tried to make in the past? Tell a partner.

D 🔊 **Make predictions.** Before you listen, read the sentences. Guess the answers. Then listen and complete the definition. **CD 2 Track 16**

A New Year's resolution is a kind of personal ___*Plan*___ you make. You decide to make a ___*to chang*___ in the New Year and work very ___*hard*___ to do it.

E 🔊 💬 **Listen for details.** What are Jamal and Lea's resolutions? Write *J* for Jamal and *L* for Lea. (There are two extra.) Do you share any resolutions with Jamal or Lea? If so which one(s)? Tell a partner. **CD 2 Track 17**

___*S*___ 1. get better grades

___*L*___ 2. find a part-time job

___*J*___ 3. join a gym

___*L*___ 4. earn money

___*S*___ 5. lose weight

___*J*___ 6. gain weight

WORLD LINK

What kind of New Year's resolutions are most popular? Go online or ask your friends and family. What did you discover?

4 SPEAKING

A 🔊 Listen to the conversation. What does Zack want from Juan? How does he ask for it? **CD 2 Track 18**

ZACK: See you later, Juan. I'm going out for a while.

JUAN: OK, see you.

ZACK: Oh no!

JUAN: What?

ZACK: I forgot to go to the ATM.

JUAN: Do you need money?

ZACK: Yeah, I'd like to get a haircut this afternoon. Can I borrow $20?

JUAN: Sure, here you go.

ZACK: Thanks a lot.

B 🔄 Practice the conversation with a partner.

SPEAKING STRATEGY

C 🔄 Choose an item from the box. Ask to borrow it from your partner and give a reason. Use the Useful Expressions to help you create a conversation.

your partner's phone
some money
your partner's car
your idea: _____

> Laura, could I borrow your phone for a minute? The bus is late and I need to call my mom.

Useful Expressions
Making and responding to requests

Can / Could I borrow your phone?
    (= Is it OK if I borrow...)
Can / Could you lend me your phone?
    (= Would you please lend...)

Positive responses	Negative response
Sure. No problem. Certainly.	I'm sorry, but... (+ reason).

Speaking tip
May I... is more polite than *Can / Could I...*: *May I borrow your pen for a second?*

D 🔄 Change roles and create a new conversation.

5 GRAMMAR

A Turn to page 210. Complete the exercise. Then do **B–E** below.

Like to	Would like to
Sentence 1: I **like to** spend time in the Outback.	*Sentence 2*: I'**d like to** spend time in the Outback.

B Read the sentences. Which ones are logical follow-up statements to Sentence 1 above? Which ones could follow Sentence 2? Why? Discuss your answers with a partner.

1 a. I always enjoy my time there.

2 b. I hope to go someday.

2 c. It looks like a beautiful place.

1 d. I'm planning to go again next year.

1 e. It's a lot of fun.

2 f. People say it's a lot of fun.

C Read the questions. Then circle the correct words to complete each answer.

1. What do you usually do on the weekend?

   (I like to) / I'd like to relax.

2. Why are you studying for the TOEFL exam?

   I like to / (I'd like to) find a job overseas.

3. What's your New Year's resolution?

   I like to / (I'd like to) get in shape.

4. Why is Mike gaining weight?

   (He likes to) / He'd like to eat desserts.

5. How was your trip to Brazil?

   We loved it! We like to / (We'd like to) visit again.

6. Do your parents both work?

   Yes, but they like to / (they'd like to) retire soon.

D Write sentences about yourself. Use these topics and start each sentence with *I like to* or *I'd like to*.

1. your free time

2. after graduation

3. your favorite TV show

4. fun things you do in your city

5. plans for next summer

6. changes in your life

E Take turns talking about your answers in **D** with a partner.

The Australian Outback

6 COMMUNICATION

A 🔄 Look at the lists of bad habits and bad qualities below. Add one more idea to each list. Tell your partner.

BAD HABITS	BAD QUALITIES
I...	I'm...
bite my nails.	messy.
spend too much money.	lazy.
eat a lot of junk food.	late all the time.
talk on the phone too much.	careless with money.
watch too much TV.	too laid-back.
your idea: _____	your idea: _____

> ℹ️ A **habit** is something you do regularly: *I check my email when I get up.* A **quality** is something that describes your personality: *I'm a serious student.*

B 🔄 Look at the pictures with a partner. What bad habits and bad qualities do these people have?

C 🔄 **Student A:** Imagine that you are the person in Picture 1 above. First, tell your partner about your bad habits and bad qualities. Then tell your partner how you want to change. Ask your partner for advice.

Student B: Listen to your partner. Suggest ways that he or she can change.

A: I like to go shopping, but I spend too much money.

B: You should try to save some money—a little bit each month.

A: I'd like to save money, but I have a lot of bills. What can I do?

B: Well, don't use your credit cards. It's...

D 🔄 Switch roles and do another role play. **Student B** is the person in Picture 2 above.

Rina, Nick, and Sarah are graduating from college.

1 VOCABULARY

A 🔊 Look at the photo and read the students' comments below. Answer the questions with a partner.

> *Rina:* I'm **getting ready** to graduate next week. I **applied for** four jobs, but so far… nothing. I know **it takes time**, but I want to get a job soon.
>
> *Nick:* My **goal** is to **become** a doctor. So I'm going to go to medical school after graduation.
>
> *Sarah:* I'm so glad school is over! I want to **take it easy**. I'm going to **take** the summer **off** and travel.

1. What are all the students getting ready to do?

2. Whose goal is to:

   a. go back to school? _Nick_

   b. get a job? _Rina_

   c. relax and not work? _Sarah_

Word Bank
get ready = prepare (to do something)
take it easy = relax
take (time) off = stop working

B 🔊 Complete the sentences about yourself. Then tell a partner your answers.

1. I'm getting ready to ~~tak Summer~~ _class_ soon.

2. This summer, I plan to _____.

   a. take it easy   c. travel

   (b.) work or study   d. other: _____

3. After I finish school, my goal is to _____.

   a. take a month off and do nothing   c. travel

   b. apply for jobs   (d.) other: _go to medical school_

4. It takes ___Four___ year(s) to graduate from college in my country.

ℹ️ *It takes* + time expression + infinitive
It takes time <u>to get</u> a job.
It took four years <u>to finish</u> college.

> I'm getting ready to take the TOEFL soon.

2 LISTENING

A 🎤 Who is your favorite singer? What did he or she do in the last couple of months? Check (✓) the boxes. Then tell a partner.

☑ went on tour   ☐ appeared on TV

☐ recorded an album   ☐ your idea: _____

B 🔊 **Listen for details.** Listen to the interview with Yeliz, a singer. Circle the correct words to complete the sentences. **CD 2 Track 19**

1. Yeliz is in ⟨Los Angeles⟩ / Istanbul now. She lives in ⟨Istanbul⟩ / Scotland.
2. She hardly ever / ⟨often⟩ travels.
3. Yeliz is getting ready to take time off / ⟨put out a new album.⟩
4. Then in two months, she plans to take it easy / ⟨go on tour.⟩
5. Yeliz ⟨plans to⟩ / doesn't plan to quit singing in school.

C 🔊 **Understand a speaker's attitude.** Listen again. How does Yeliz feel about these things? Circle your answers and write one key word that supports each answer. **CD 2 Track 19**

How does Yeliz feel about…

1. traveling?   She ⟨likes⟩ / doesn't like it.   key word: _It's fun_
2. recording?   She ⟨likes⟩ / doesn't like it.   key word: _It's interesting_
3. school?   She ⟨likes⟩ / doesn't like it.   key word: _She loves it_

D 🎤 Do you think Yeliz's life is interesting? Why or why not? Tell a partner.

3 READING

A LIFETIME DREAM

A high school student from Sudan and a teacher from China tell about their hopes for the future.

A ✦ **Make predictions.** Look at the title of the reading and the photo. Guess: What are these people's future goals? Tell a partner. Then read the passage to check your ideas.

B **Read for details.** Read the passage again and complete the chart.

	Wang	Hicham
1. Where does he or she live?	Beijing	London
2. What does he or she do?	teaching	student
3. What is his or her goal?	make film	Pro soccer player
4. What's stopping him or her?	money	parents

C **Scan for information.** Quickly find each of the activities below in the reading. Is the person doing it now? Check *N*. Is it the person's future goal? Check *F*. Underline the sentence in the reading that helped you choose your answer.

Yi Wang

1. teach at a university — N ☑ F ☐
2. write a film — N ☑ F ☐
3. go to film festivals — N ☐ F ☑

Hicham Nassir

4. live in London — N ☑ F ☐
5. play professional soccer — N ☐ F ☑
6. practice every day — N ☑ F ☐

D ✦ Role-play a dialog between Wang and Hicham. Ask the questions in **B**. At the end, give some advice: How can the person make his or her goal happen?

> Hi, I'm Yi Wang.

> Hi, I'm Hicham Nassir.

> Where are you from, Hicham?

> I'm from Sudan.

Hicham Nassir

Seventeen-year-old Hicham Nassir is getting ready for a soccer match with his teammates. Hicham, a student and his school's best player, is a native of Sudan. He now lives in London with his family.

"My parents are worried. They want me to go to college and major in business or law," he explains. "They want me to get a job as a lawyer or work as a businessman. I understand them, but I want to become a pro soccer player. This summer, I'm going to practice really hard every day."

And what about his parents? "I hope they change their minds,"[1] says Hicham. "I want to play soccer professionally. It's my dream."

Yi Wang

"At the moment, I'm teaching chemistry at a university in Beijing. It's a good job, but my dream is to make films," says 29-year-old Yi Wang. "In China, young artists move to Beijing from all over the country. Many of them are painters, writers, and actors. I'd like to take some time off and make a film about their lives and their work."

Wang is writing a film now with help from her friends. But it isn't easy. "At the moment, the biggest problem is money," explains Wang. "We don't have much."

But this isn't going to stop Wang and her partners. They are ambitious. "First, we're going to make this movie. Then we'd like to show it in China and, maybe someday, at film festivals around the world. It's going to take time, but I think we can do it."

[1] If you *change your mind,* you change your opinion about something.

4 GRAMMAR

A Turn to page 211. Complete the exercises. Then do **B** and **C** below.

The Future with *be going to*					
Subject + *be*	**(*not*)**	***going to***	**Verb**		**Future time expression**
I'm	(not)	**going to**	start	college	this fall. / in August. next month. / after graduation.

Yes / No and *Wh-* questions						**Answers**	
	Are	you	**going to**	start	college?	Yes, I am.	No, I'm not.
When	are					(I'm going to start) in August.	

B Answer the questions in the chart by checking (✓) the correct box for each. Then add one more.

Amina

In the future, are you going to...	Yes, I am.	Maybe.	Probably not.	No, I'm not.
study English?	✓	✓		
take the TOEFL exam?				✓
move to another city?	✓			
get married?				✓
apply for a job?	✓			
visit another country?	✓			
learn another language?	✓			
start your own business?	✓			
take time off?	✓			
Uneversity ?		✓		

C ↻ Take turns asking and answering the questions in **B** with a partner. Then ask one follow-up *Wh-* question with *be going to.* Use the models below.

A: In the future, are you going to move to another city?

B: Yes, maybe.

A: Really? Where are you going to move?

B: Tokyo. I want to get a job there.

A: Are you going to move to another city?

B: Probably not.

A: Why not?

B: I like my hometown. It's comfortable here.

5 WRITING

A Read about one person's goal. Notice the words in bold used to introduce new topics. Then answer the questions below.

> ## My Goal
>
> My goal is to run in the São Paulo International Marathon next year. I'm going to do three things to get ready. **First**, I'm going to buy some new shoes. I need good shoes for running. **Also**, I'm going to run every day for ten months. A marathon is 42 kilometers, and a runner needs a lot of practice. **Finally**, I'm going to quit eating junk food and start eating more fruit and vegetables. A runner needs to be healthy. It's going to be hard, but I can do it!

1. What is the person's goal?

2. He is going to do three things to make his goal happen. What are they?

i The writer explains each of his three ideas with an extra sentence.

B What is one of your goals? Complete the sentences with your ideas. Then use your notes to write a paragraph.

My goal is to…

To do this, first, I'm going to…

Also, I'm going to…

Finally, I'm going to…

It's going to be hard, but I'm going to do it!

C Exchange papers with a partner.

1. Answer questions 1 and 2 in **A** about your partner.

2. Circle any mistakes in your partner's writing. Then return the paper to him or her.

The São Paulo International Marathon

6 COMMUNICATION

A Prepare a short talk.

1. Practice with a partner: Use your notes in Writing to talk about your goal. Do not just read your paragraph.

2. Find photos or a video clip to use in your presentation.

B Work in a small group. Give your presentation.

1. When you listen, answer questions 1 and 2 in Writing **A**.

2. Can the speaker do anything else to make his or her goal happen? Tell the group.

1 STORYBOARD

A Rolf is telling Brigit about his trip. Look at the pictures and complete the conversation. More than one answer may be possible for each blank.

B Practice the conversation with a partner. Then change roles and practice again.

2 SEE IT AND SAY IT

A 🔄 Talk about the picture with a partner. Answer these questions.

- Where are these people?
- What are they doing?
- Look at the different ads. What are they about?

Now answer these questions.

- How is the traffic and pollution in your city?
- How often do you take public transportation?
- What other forms of transportation do you take?
- Ask your partner one more question about the picture.

B 🔄 With a partner, choose one pair of people in the picture. Role-play a conversation between the two people.

3 THEY'RE GOING TO GET MARRIED!

A Look at the wedding announcement below. Two people are getting married. Think of a man and a woman. They can be famous people or other people you know. Complete the information about them.

> ## We're Getting Married!
>
> Name: Name:
>
> Job: Job:
>
> Age: Age:
>
> Personality: Personality:

B Work alone. You are going to interview the man and woman in **A** using the questions below. Read the questions and complete the last three with *be going to*.

- When did you meet?
- How did you meet?
- When are you going to get married?
- Who are you going to invite to the wedding?
- Where _____?
- How much _____?
- How many _____?

C Conduct the interview with a partner.

Student A: You are one of the people in **A**. Answer the reporter's questions. Use your imagination.

Student B: You are a newspaper reporter. Use your questions to interview the man or woman. Take notes.

D Switch roles and do the interview again. **Student A** is now the reporter and **Student B** is one of the people in **A**.

E Share some of your interview notes with another pair.

> I interviewed Bruno Mars. He's dating Mia, our classmate! They're going to get married next month!

> Really? How did they meet?

4 LISTENING

A 🔊 Look at each photo. Then listen to the four sentences for each one. Circle the letter of the sentence that best describes the photo. **CD 2 Track 21**

1.

A   B   C   D

2.

A   B   C   D

3.

A   B   C   D

4.

A   B   C   D

10 HEALTH

Look at the photo. Answer the questions.

1 What is this woman doing?

2 Is this activity good or bad for you? Why?

3 Imagine your friend wants to do this activity. Give one piece of advice.

UNIT GOALS

1 Identify parts of the body

2 Talk about health problems

3 Make requests and commands

4 Describe causes of stress and explain how to deal with them

Ultra trail runner Rory Bosio runs in Iceland's Lakagígar lava fields.

Dr. Ellsworth Wareham mows his lawn.

1 VIDEO Centenarian's Guide to Longevity

A   Read this information about Dr. Fraser and his study. What do you think Ellsworth Wareham does differently in his life? Discuss with a partner.

Dr. Gary Fraser studied 34,000 older people. He found that some people, like Dr. Ellsworth Wareham, were very healthy: they outlived other men by 9.5 years.

B   Read the sentences and then watch the video about Dr. Wareham. Circle *T* for true and *F* for false.

1. Dr. Wareham retired at a young age.	T	(F)
2. Eating nuts and exercising are important for a healthy life.	(T)	F
3. Climbing stairs 40 times a week helps you to stay healthy.	T	(F)
4. Dr. Wareham lives a stressful life.	T	(F)
5. Dr. Wareham says, "You do the best you can."	(T)	F
6. Dr. Wareham says, "You can take control of your life."	(T)	F

C   What do you think of Dr. Wareham's life and the advice in **B**? Tell a partner.

2 VOCABULARY

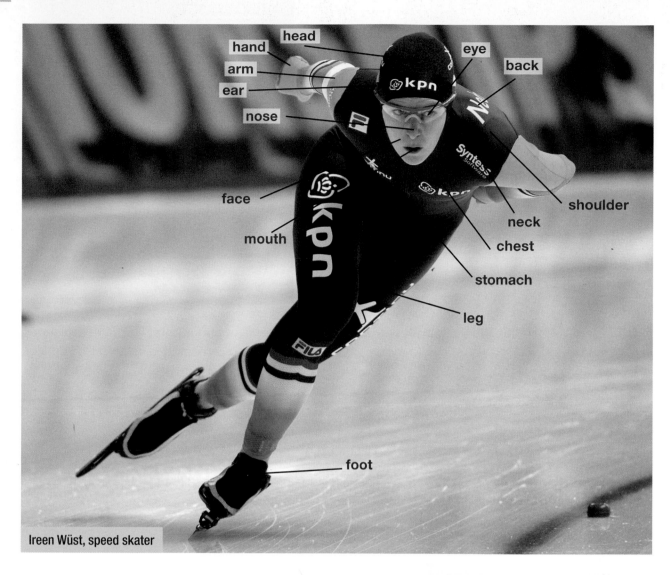

head
hand
arm
ear
nose
eye
back
face
mouth
shoulder
neck
chest
stomach
leg
foot

Ireen Wüst, speed skater

A 🔄 With a partner, practice saying the words for parts of the body.

B 🔄 Can you name each part of the body without looking at the words? Tell your partner.

C 🔄 Close your books. Tell a partner things to do. Use body parts from the list.

> Touch your nose.

> Point to your right shoulder.

> Stand on your left leg.

Word Bank
Opposites
broad ↔ **narrow** (shoulders)
long ↔ **short** (arms / legs)
big / **large** ↔ **little** / **small** (eyes / nose)
muscular (body / arms / legs)

WORLD LINK

Go online and learn more about Ireen Wüst. Where is she from? How many medals did she win? Why do you think she was successful?

3 LISTENING

A 🔊 **Pronunciation: Vowel length with voiced and voiceless consonants.** Say the words. Then listen and repeat. How are the vowel sounds different in the group A and group B words? **CD 2 Track 22**

A	B
bag	back
phase	face
feed	feet
made	mate
have	half
Ms.	Miss
save	safe

ℹ️ Vowels before voiced consonants are longer than those before voiceless ones.

B 🔊 **Pronunciation: Vowel length with voiced and voiceless consonants.** Read the sentences. Then listen and repeat. Pay attention to the length of the vowel sound in the underlined words. **CD 2 Track 23**

1. OK, <u>Ms.</u> Jones, where are you now?
2. I <u>have</u> a security camera in my home.
3. And please hurry! I don't feel <u>safe</u>.
4. Well, it's kind of dark. And I can only see his <u>back</u>.

C 🔄 **Make predictions.** Before you listen, look at the photo and reread the sentences in **B**. What do you think the listening is going to be about? Discuss with a partner.

D 🔊 **Listen for details.** Listen to the phone call and complete the information about the caller. **CD 2 Track 24**

First name: _Ann_   Home address: _22 lake St._

Last name: _Jones_

E 🔊 **Listen for details.** Listen. Circle your answer(s). **CD 2 Track 25**

1. The caller is _____.
   a. at home   b. calling the police   c.) worried
2. The man is _____.
   a.) tall   b. large   c.) young
3. The man _____.
   a.) turns on the TV   b. turns off the lights   c. eats popcorn
4. In the end, the woman feels _____.
   a. worried   b. scared   c.) embarrassed

F 🔄 When there's an emergency (car accident, fire, etc.), people in the United States call 911. What number do you call? Have you ever called that number? Tell a partner.

4 SPEAKING

A 🔊 Listen to the conversation. What's wrong with Jon? Check (✓) the box(es). **CD 2 Track 26**

☑ His head hurts.   ☐ His back hurts.   ☐ He's tired.

MIA: Hello?

JON: Hi, Mia. It's Jon.

MIA: Jon! Where are you? It's 7:30. The movie starts in 20 minutes.

JON: Sorry to call so late, but I can't meet you tonight.

MIA: Really?

JON: Yeah, I don't feel well.

MIA: What's wrong?

JON: I have a headache, and I'm really tired.

MIA: Oh, sorry to hear that. Well, get some rest, and I'll call you in the morning.

JON: OK. Talk to you then.

B 🔄 Practice the conversation with a partner.

SPEAKING STRATEGY

C What's wrong with Jenna? Match each pair of sentences to one picture.

1. She has a backache.
   Her back hurts.

2. She has a stomachache.
   Her stomach hurts.

3. She has a sore throat.
   Her throat hurts.

4. She has a fever and a bad cold. She has a temperature.

D 🔄 With a partner, take turns practicing the conversation in **A** again. Then use the words you just learned in **C** to make a new conversation.

E 🔄 Role-play with a partner. You have plans to meet a friend, but you don't feel well. Call your friend and explain the situation. Use the Useful Expressions to help you.

> I'm sorry, but I can't go to the party. I have a bad cold.

> Oh, no! I'm sorry to hear that. Get some rest!

Useful Expressions
Talking about health problems
What's wrong? / What's the matter?
I don't feel well.
I'm sick.
I have a / an (fever).
My (leg) hurts.
Speaking tip
When you hear bad news, you can respond with *(I'm) sorry to hear that.* or *Oh, that's too bad.*

F 🔄 Change roles and practice again.

5 GRAMMAR

A Turn to page 212. Complete the exercise. Then do **B** and **C** below.

Imperatives		
Don't	**Base form**	
	Take	a break.
Don't	work	too hard.
	Get	some rest.

B Use the verbs in the box to complete the health tips. Use affirmative or negative forms of the imperative. You will use one word in the box twice.

drink   eat   give   go   sleep   take   wash

Health tips: The common cold

To stay healthy:

1. _____Take_____ vitamins.
2. _____Don't eat_____ a lot of junk food.
3. _____Sleep_____ for 8–9 hours a night.
4. _____Wash_____ your hands often.
5. _____drink_____ a cup of green tea daily.
6. _____Don't eat_____ too much soda. Water is better.

If you have a cold:

7. _____Don't go_____ to school or work.
8. _____Take_____ an aspirin for pain and fever.
9. _____Don't got_____ aspirin to children under 12! It's dangerous.
10. _____Eat_____ a bowl of chicken soup.

C  Work with a partner. Read the list and add your own idea to it. Then imagine you have one of these health problems. Ask your partner for advice.

1. I can't sleep at night.
2. I have a stomachache.
3. My legs hurt after I run.
4. Your idea: _____

> I can't sleep at night.

> Don't drink coffee in the evening!

Exercise helps you stay healthy, too.

6 COMMUNICATION

A This poster gives advice. Read it and then answer the questions.

1. Have you ever seen a poster like this?
2. Where do you see posters like this in your city?
3. What does the poster tell people to do?
4. What other ideas can you add to the poster?

B Read the ideas for poster titles. With a partner, write another idea.

> Fight pollution in our city!
>
> Eat healthy, live longer.
>
> Get in shape today!
>
> Protect your skin this summer!
>
> Don't drink and drive.
>
> Your idea: _____

C Use one of the titles from **B** to create a poster on a separate piece of paper. Think of what advice to give.

D **Group A:** Present your poster to another pair. Discuss it with them.

Group B: What do you like most about the poster? Can you add one piece of advice to the poster?

Change roles and repeat.

LESSON B STRESS

ZOE: I'm **stressed**. I have three exams and two papers to write this month. I don't **have time** to do it all and I have no time to **relax**!

MIGUEL: I have a **stressful** job, and I work long hours. In the past, I was **full of energy**. But now, I'm always **low on energy** and tired, so I drink a lot of coffee. Then I can't sleep at night.

1 VOCABULARY

A 🔁 Work with a partner. Answer the questions.

1. Find the word *stress* in your dictionary. Is stress good or bad?

2. Why is each person above stressed?

Word Bank
Opposites
be full of ↔ be low on (energy)
stressed ↔ relaxed
stressful ↔ relaxing

B 🔁 What can each person do? Match the ideas (a–d) with a person. Some ideas might match both people. Explain your ideas with your partner.

To **deal with** stress, Zoe / Miguel should…

a. **reduce** (lower) the amount of coffee he or she drinks.

b. **take time** to relax every day.

c. **make a schedule** and do some work every day.

> Miguel should exercise more. Exercise reduces stress and gives you energy.

d. exercise more.

C 🔁 Are the sentences below true for you? Tell your partner.

1. Usually, I'm full of energy.
2. Usually, I have time to do all my work.
3. School or work is stressful for me.
4. To reduce stress, I listen to music.

2 LISTENING

A Look at the photos. Do you ever drink or take these things? If yes, how often?

> **Word Bank**
>
> You *drink* liquids like water.
> You *take* vitamins / aspirin / medicine.

B 🔊 **Listen for gist.** What is the advertisement about? Listen and circle the correct photo above. **CD 2 Track 27**

C 🔊 **Listen for details.** Read the sentences. Then listen and complete each blank with one or two words. **CD 2 Track 28**

One person's opinion about the item

1. "Before I took _____vitamin_____, I was living an _____unhappy_____ life."
2. "I felt _____tired_____ all the time."
3. "Now I'm _____full of_____ energy, and I can deal with _____stress_____ better."
4. "I _____love_____ these… and you will, too!"

More information about the item

5. They are selling _____quickly_____.
6. They cost $ __29__.95.

D 💬 **Draw conclusions.** Look at your answers in **B** and **C**. Would you buy this product? Why or why not? Tell a partner.

E 💬 Role-play. Imagine you are low on energy. Your partner gives you some advice.

A: Hey, Marta, what's the matter?
B: Oh, I'm kind of low on energy.
A: That's too bad. Why?
B: I'm always sitting and studying in the library. I don't exercise.
A: Well, I have an idea…

3 READING

A **Make predictions.** Read the title and the first paragraph.

1. What is the student's problem?

2. What can the student do? Make a list of some ideas.

3. Read the entire passage and check your answers in 2.

B **Read for main ideas.** Write each sentence below in the correct place in the reading (1, 2, 3, or 4).

Eat well.   Get a study partner.

Don't do too much.   Stop and relax.

C **Infer meaning.** Find the phrases in italics in the reading. Complete each sentence.

1. Tip #1: If you *wait until the last minute*, you do something early / very late.

2. Tip #2: If you *take a break*, you stop / keep working for a short time.

3. Tip #4: If you are *under pressure*, you're feeling very stressed / relaxed.

D  **Understand a writer's opinion.** Which sentences would the writer of the tips agree with? Check (✓) them. Explain your answers to a partner.

☐ It's best to study a little bit each day.

☐ The best hours for studying are from 11 PM to 1 AM.

☐ Breaks are good, but it's best to stay indoors.

☐ Drinking coffee helps you remember information better.

☐ It's good to tell a study partner your feelings.

E Talk with a partner. Do you agree with the study tips in the reading? Why or why not? Do you ever do these things?

HOW TO DEAL WITH
STUDY STRESS

I'm getting ready to take the university entrance exam. To prepare, I'm studying six hours a day. I want to do well, but I'm really stressed these days. I can't sleep. What can I do?

1. _____ Don't wait until the last minute, or just a day or two before the exam. Make a study schedule for yourself, but don't study too much in one day. You remember more by studying one hour each day for six days than six hours in one day. Also, don't study late at night. We often forget information studied then.

2. _____ You learn best when you study for two hours and then stop. Every hour, take a break for 10 to 15 minutes. Go for a walk. Exercise is a great way to reduce stress.

3. _____ Don't eat a lot of sugar or drink beverages with a lot of caffeine, like coffee or energy drinks. Eat foods high in vitamin B (for example, eggs, yogurt, green vegetables, tofu, and rice). These things give you energy and help you think better.

4. _____ A study partner can help you practice for the test. When you're under pressure and nervous about the exam, you can talk to your partner. This can reduce stress, too.

People study and read at the British Library, London, England.

4 GRAMMAR

A Turn to page 213. Complete the exercises. Then do **B** and **C** below.

When Clauses	
***When* clause**	**Result clause**
When(ever) I drink coffee,	I can't sleep.
Result clause	***When* clause**
I can't sleep	when(ever) I drink coffee.

B Complete the sentences with your own information.

1. When I don't feel well, *I take aspirin and drink tea* _____.

2. When I meet new people, _____.

3. When I don't understand something in English, _____.

4. When I have a lot to do, I _____.

5. When I (don't) take time to _____, I _____.

6. I get impatient when _____.

7. I feel happy when _____.

8. I feel _____ when _____.

C 🔄 Take turns saying the sentences in **B**. For each sentence, your partner asks you one question.

> When I don't feel well, I take aspirin and drink tea.

> Really? Does it help?

5 WRITING

A Read about a student's problem and one person's advice. Answer the questions.

1. What is the student stressed about? Why is he stressed?

2. What advice does the other person give? Is it good advice?

Q: *I feel stressed when I think about graduation. I'm a senior in college. Soon, I have to get a job. When I think about that, I feel nervous. What can I do?*

A: When you feel stressed, try these two things: First, make a list of your goals. What do you want to do in the future? Write three ideas. Then talk to Ms. Kim, the school counselor. Show her your goals. She can give you some job advice. She can also help you plan for the future. Try these two things. They can reduce your stress.

B Read the list of stressful situations in the box and choose one. Write your sentence on a piece of paper. Explain why the situation is stressful for you.

C 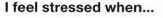 Exchange papers with a partner.

1. Read your partner's problem.

2. What can your partner do? Write a reply.
Give two pieces of advice. Use the example in **A** to help you.

D Give your reply to your partner. Read his or her ideas for your problem. Are they helpful?

6 COMMUNICATION

A Choose a situation below and make a one-minute role play about it with a partner. Use at least two *when* clauses in your conversation.

Student A: Explain your problem.

You...

- had a fight with a friend.
- have a lot of homework but don't have time to do it all.
- are under a lot of pressure at work.
- like a guy or girl, but you're nervous to talk to the person.

Student B: Give your partner some advice.

> I have too much work. When it's time to go, I still have so much to do!

> Really? Maybe you should talk to your boss.

> When I do...

B Perform your role play for another pair. When you listen, answer these questions.

1. Why is the person stressed?
2. What advice did his or her partner give?
3. Is it good advice?
4. Can you think of other advice?

C Repeat **A** and **B**. This time, choose a new situation and change roles.

11 ACHIEVEMENT

Look at the photo. Answer the questions.

1 What is this person doing?

2 What important thing did he do?

3 Could you do something like this?

UNIT GOALS

1 Talk about past and present achievements

2 Offer and respond to compliments

3 Talk about taking risks

4 Describe a challenging experience

Austrian skydiver Felix Baumgartner prepares to jump over 39 kilometers (128,000 feet) to Earth from a balloon. His jump broke a record at the time.

1 **VIDEO** Caine's Arcade

Word Bank

arcade = a place where people pay money to play games

A Read the information and then answer the questions with a partner: Who is Caine? What did he make? What's his problem?

Caine is a nine-year-old boy. His father works at a garage, and Caine spent his summer vacation there. Caine had a lot of free time, so he decided to use old boxes to make an arcade. There was only one problem: not many people came to the garage, so Caine didn't have any customers.

B Watch the video. Choose the correct words to complete the sentences.

1. Caine's first game was a basketball / soccer game.

2. To play the arcade games, it cost one dollar for four turns or two dollars for 50 / 500 turns.

3. Caine didn't have any customers. He never got excited / discouraged.

4. Nirvan had a plan to invite a few friends / everyone in the city to Caine's arcade.

5. When Caine saw all the people, he was very worried / excited.

C With a partner, plan a new game for Caine's Arcade. Explain your game and how to play it to the class.

2 VOCABULARY

A 🔂 Read this profile of Germán Garmendia. Answer the questions with a partner.

1. What is Germán famous for?
2. Why is he **successful**?

HI, I'M GERMÁN!

Germán Garmendia is a **talented** Chilean comic. His online video channel, *Hola, Soy Germán*, has more than 20 million fans worldwide. They enjoy his funny videos. The videos **get** millions of **hits**.

What is the secret to Germán's **success**? First, he **posts** new **videos** frequently. Second, he **has a** natural **ability** to tell jokes. Third, he can make everyday life events seem very funny.

B 🔂 Discuss the questions with a partner.

1. What funny videos do you watch online?
2. Name a famous video star you know.
3. How many hits do his or her videos have? How many fans does he or she have?
4. Why is this person successful? Do you think he or she is talented?

Go online and watch a minute of one of Germán's videos. Why do you think he has so many fans?

3 LISTENING

Word Bank
audition = a short performance to see if a person is talented enough for a show
contest = competition or game
talent show = contest where people perform to win a prize

A Think of a well-known talent show or contest on TV. Do you watch it? Why or why not? Complete the information below and share your answers with a partner.

Name of contest: _Sitari Afghan_ ☑ I watch it. ☐ I don't watch it.

Reasons: 1. _Becuse it maks me happy._

2. _Becuse I like the singing._

B **Listen for details.** You are going to hear an interview about an audition for a talent show. Listen to the first part of the interview and match the adjectives to the things or people they describe. You will hear one of the adjectives twice. **CD 2 Track 30**

1. beautiful _a_
2. talented _c_
3. young _c_
4. excited _d_
5. popular _b_
6. ambitious _d_
7. not confident _d_

a. Essex Theater
b. *Idol Singer*
c. people in line
d. Cindy Gomez

C **Listen to sequence events.** Now listen to the next part of the interview. When do these events happen? Put them in order. **CD 2 Track 31**

_7_ audition

_4_ come back the next day

_6_ appear on *Idol Singer*

_3_ get a ticket

_2_ have an interview

_5_ wait in line for one hour

_1_ wait in line for two hours

D Imagine you are going to audition for *Idol Singer* in five minutes. What song are you going to sing? How do you feel right now? Tell a partner.

4 SPEAKING

A 🔊 Tyler and Ayumi are at a party. Listen to the conversation. What does Tyler say about Ayumi's painting? **CD 2 Track 32**

AYUMI: Hi, Tyler. Are you enjoying yourself?

TYLER: Yeah, I really am. What a great art show.

AYUMI: Yeah, it's really interesting.

TYLER: So... which painting is yours?

AYUMI: This one... right over here.

TYLER: Wow. I like it a lot.

AYUMI: Really? Thank you.

TYLER: How long did it take you to finish it?

AYUMI: About two months.

B 🔁 Practice the conversation with a partner.

SPEAKING STRATEGY

C 🔁 Read the Useful Expressions. With a partner, write one follow-up question for each compliment and response.

Useful Expressions		
Offering compliments about things	**Responses**	**Follow-up questions**
Nice haircut!		Where did you get it done?
Cool glasses!		Were they expensive?
That's an interesting story. That's amazing!	Thanks!	
I like your jacket a lot.	Thank you.	
What a great painting!	That's nice of you to say.	
Offering compliments about abilities		
You can speak English really well!		
Speaking tip		
You can add information to your compliment to make it more specific: *Nice dress. I like the pattern.*		

D 🔁 With a partner, create conversations for situations 1 and 2 below. Offer a compliment and ask follow-up questions.

Situation 1
Student A: You're a guitarist. You wrote a new song and you're practicing it.
Student B: You hear your partner practicing a song. You like it. You think your partner plays well.

Situation 2
Student B: You're wearing a new sweater. It didn't cost a lot of money.
Student A: Your partner is wearing a new sweater. You think it's cool.

5 GRAMMAR

A Turn to page 214. Complete the exercise. Then do **B–F** below.

Using *can* for Ability			
Subject	**Modal verb**	**Base form**	
I / You / He / She / It / We / You / They	**can / can't** **could / couldn't**	sing	well.
	Modal verb	**Base form**	
	Can you	sing	well?

> ℹ️ You can also use *know how to* to talk about abilities.

> ℹ️ Do not use *could* to talk about past abilities if it's a one-time achievement. Use *was able to* instead: ~~I could win first place in the contest.~~ *I was able to win first place in the contest.*

B 🔊 **Pronunciation: *Can / can't.*** Listen to the examples. Then listen and repeat 1–4.
CD 2 Track 33

I can sing well.

1. I can sing a song in English.
2. I can say *I love you* in three languages.

I can't sing well.

3. I can't dance.
4. I can't draw a picture with my eyes closed.

C Complete the sentences with *can, can't, could, couldn't,* or *be able to* (where necessary).

1. You ___Can___ be successful. Just work hard.
2. Yesterday, I ___couldn't___ finish the test early.
3. My sister's baby ___could___ read by age two.
4. ___Could___ you speak English when you were little?
5. I ___can___ speak Chinese, but I ___can't___ read or write it.

D 🔁 Add your own question to the list below. Ask a partner the questions.

Can you…

1. sing a song in English?
2. draw a picture with your eyes closed?
3. dance?
4. say *I love you* in three languages?
5. count quickly from 20 back to zero in English?
6. _____

E 👥 Get into a small group. Follow the steps below.

- Use the ideas in **D**. Talk to another person about his or her ability. Say, *I bet you can't…*
- If the person can do it, he or she gets a point. If he or she can't, you get a point.
- Take turns. The person with the most points is the winner.

> I bet you can't sing a song in English.

F 👥 What is something you can do now but couldn't do in the past? How did you learn it? Discuss it with your group.

6 COMMUNICATION

A Read about the TV show *Talent Search!* Do you know any other shows like this one?

Talent Search! is a popular TV show. Talented people go on the show and try to win prizes. Some people sing or dance. Others tell jokes, do magic tricks, or act. The audience chooses the best person.

B Imagine that you are going to be on *Talent Search!* Complete the form about yourself.

1. Name: _____

2. Where are you from? _____

3. What's your special talent? _____

4. How did you learn to do that? _____

5. What exactly are you going to do on the show? _____
_____

C 🔁 Get together with a partner and ask him or her the questions in **B**. Write his or her answers on a piece of paper.

What's your special talent?

Well, I can ride a unicycle!

That's amazing! How did you learn to do that?

I practiced every day for six months. At first, I couldn't do it at all, but then...

D 🔗 You and your partner should join two other pairs. Imagine that you are a *Talent Search!* announcer. Introduce your partner to the group. Use your notes from **C**.

Presenting a talented young man from Mexico City—Ivan Perez! He can...

E 🔗 Who has the most interesting talent in your group? Why?

Risk-takers...

- are brave people. They aren't **afraid** to try **dangerous** things, like rock climbing.

- like a **challenge** (something difficult).

- are **curious**. They like to meet new people and learn new things.

- are **adventurous**. They might start their own company, for example. It might do well or it might not, but risk-takers still **take a chance** and try.

1 VOCABULARY

A Read the descriptions of *risk-takers* above. Then circle the true answers below. Explain your ideas to a partner.

A risk-taker might...

1. move to another country.

2. talk to a new person at a party.

3. do the same job all his or her life.

4. want to do the activity on page 154.

> A risk-taker might.... They are curious about other people.

Word Bank
Opposites
adventurous ↔ **careful**
afraid ↔ **brave**
curious ↔ **uninterested**
dangerous / risky ↔ **safe**
take a chance ↔ **play it safe**

B Look at the photo above. Then complete the sentences below with your own information.

1. Usually, I am / am not afraid to take a chance and try new things.

2. The activity in the photo looks very dangerous / kind of fun.

3. I like a challenge / things to be easy.

4. I'm curious about / not very interested in other people.

> Yes, I am. I'm not afraid to try new things.

C Are you an adventurous person? Use your answers in **B** to explain to a partner.

2 LISTENING

You can take <u>one</u> of the items above: the $10 or a box. In one of the boxes, maybe there is more money than $10. But maybe there isn't. What do you do? Do you play it safe and take the $10, or do you take a chance and choose a box?

A Read the information above. Then check your answer below.

I'm going to take the _____.

☐ money   ☐ small box   ☑ medium box   ☐ large box

B 🔊 **Make and check predictions.** Read the sentences and guess the answers. Then listen and check your answers. **CD 2 Track 34**

	the money	the small box	the medium box	the large box
1. It's best to choose…	☑	☐	☐	☐
2. Careful people usually choose…	☐	☐	☑	☐
3. Adventurous people choose…	☐	☑	☐	☑

C 🔊 **Listen for details.** Read the sentences. Then listen and write a word in each blank. **CD 2 Track 35**

It was (1.) ___best___ to take a (2.) ___the money___ because you were told: "Maybe there is more (3.) ___money___ and maybe there isn't." It wasn't (4.) ___certain___. And for this reason, it was not (5.) ___good___ to take a chance.

D 🔁 Answer the questions with a partner.

1. What did you choose in **A**?

2. Was it better to choose the money or a box? Use your answers in **C** to explain.

3 READING

A **Make predictions.** Look at the photo and read the title and the first sentence in the first paragraph. Answer the questions.

1. What is this man's job?
2. He did something risky. What was it? Guess: Was this experience hard?

B **Read for details.** Read the entire article. Choose the correct answers below. Underline the information in the reading that helped you choose your answers.

1. Irving flies because _____.
   a. it's a good job
   b. he likes the feeling of flying
2. Irving didn't go back to Japan because _____.
   a. he didn't have enough gas
   b. his plane stopped
3. The radio pilots asked for Irving's parents' phone number because they _____.
   a. thought Irving might die
   b. wanted to help Irving
4. Irving says the difficult flying experience _____.
   a. taught him a lot   b. was exciting
5. Which sentence would Irving agree with?
   a. It's always better to play it safe. You don't always have to succeed.
   b. When things are hard, keep trying. You can succeed.

C **Infer meaning.** Complete the sentences with the best answer.

1. In line 17, *challenging* means hard / exciting / long.
2. In line 24, *give up* means continue / quit / talk.
3. In line 27, Irving says *I made it.* This means "I did something successfully / poorly / slowly."

D 🔄 Look at your answer to question 5 in **B**. Do you agree with Irving? Why or why not? Tell a partner.

DARING PILOT

1 At age 23, Barrington Irving became the youngest person to fly alone around the world—in a small plane he built himself. Since then, he started a company called Experience Aviation. It helps students learn
5 about flying and other subjects, like science and math. Students can study in the "Flying Classroom" or learn how to build cars.

Here, Barrington Irving talks about his love of flying and his flight around the world.

10 **Why do you fly?**

I love being in the air between the sky and the Earth. It's exciting, but I also feel very calm.

Are you ever afraid?

Yes, I was very afraid one time. It was during my flight
15 around the world. I had to fly from Japan to a small island called Shemya, near Alaska. The flight was challenging. It was very windy, and then there was a bad storm. At one point, the radio pilots on the ground sent me a message. They said, "You have to go back
20 to Japan." And I said, "I don't have enough fuel[1] to go back." It was risky to continue, but I took a chance and kept going. The radio pilots asked for my parents' phone number. It was the end for me, they thought, but I didn't give up. When I got to Shemya Island,
25 I had 12 minutes of fuel left.

What a frightening[2] experience!

Yes, it was, but I got to Shemya safely. I made it. And I learned a lot about flying.

[1]*Fuel* here means gas.
[2]If something is *frightening*, you feel very afraid.

Barrington Irving crouches in front of his plane.

4 GRAMMAR

A Turn to page 215. Complete the exercises. Then do **B** and **C** below.

Connecting Ideas with *because*	
Main clause	**Reason clause**
He likes to fly	**because** it's exciting.
Reason clause	**Main clause**
Because it's exciting,	he likes to fly.

Connecting Ideas with *so*	
Main clause	**Result clause**
The weather was bad,	**so** he didn't fly.

B 👥 Work in a small group. Follow the steps to play this game.

1. Write the sentence pairs in the box (1–4) on four small pieces of paper. Mix them and put them face down on the desk.

2. On three small pieces of paper, write the word *so*. On another three, write *because*. Mix these and put them face down in another pile.

3. One person begins. Turn over a word (*so* or *because*) and one of the sentence pairs. You have ten seconds to join the two sentences. If you do this correctly, you get a point.

4. When you are done, put the two pieces of paper back. Then the next person goes.

5. Play the game for 15 minutes, joining the sentences in different ways. The person with the most points wins.

> 1. I'm afraid to go in the water.
>   I don't know how to swim.
> 2. I don't smoke.
>   Smoking is dangerous.
> 3. I like to ride roller coasters.
>   They're exciting.
> 4. I want to change my major.
>   It's boring.

> I don't know how to swim, so...

C 🔄 Are any of the sentences in **B** true for you? Why or why not? Tell your partner.

> I like to ride roller coasters.

> Really? Why?

> Because I think they're exciting.

5 WRITING

A 🔁 Read the paragraph. Then answer the questions with a partner.

1. What difficult thing happened to the person? Why was it difficult?

2. Did things get better? Why or why not?

B 🔁 Review the grammar chart on page 166 about using *because* and *so*. Then look at the underlined sentences in the paragraph. Are they correct? If not, make changes. Check answers with a partner.

C Write about a challenging experience. Use an experience from the box or your own idea. Answer the questions in **A**. Use the example to help you.

D 🔁 Exchange papers with a partner. Does your partner's writing answer the questions in **A**? Circle any mistakes in your partner's writing. Then return the paper to your partner. Make corrections to your own paper.

A Challenging Experience

When I was 14, my family moved to a new city. <u>My new school was hard</u>. <u>Because I didn't know anyone</u>. Life was difficult. <u>I had no friends so, I hated school</u>. Then things changed. One day, I saw a poster for the school band. It said "Do you like jazz? Can you play the piano?" <u>I was happy, because I love jazz and piano</u>. I was also nervous, but I joined the group. I wasn't very good at first, but I didn't give up. I practiced a lot. Now these people are my friends and I like school.

Challenging experiences

moving

starting a new school or job

taking an important exam

my idea: _____

---

6 COMMUNICATION

A Look at the activities below. Add one item to the list. Which things would you like to do? Check (✓) them. Which don't you want to do? Put an X next to them.

Ten things to do before you're 70

- ☐ learn to fly a plane
- ☐ live in another country
- ☐ start your own business
- ☐ learn to play music
- ☐ be on a reality TV show
- ☐ get a tattoo
- ☐ get married
- ☐ buy an expensive car
- ☐ ride a camel in the desert
- ☐ my idea: _____

B 🔁 Get together with a partner. Ask and answer questions about your choices.

> I love flying, so I want to learn to fly a plane.

12 AT THE MOVIES

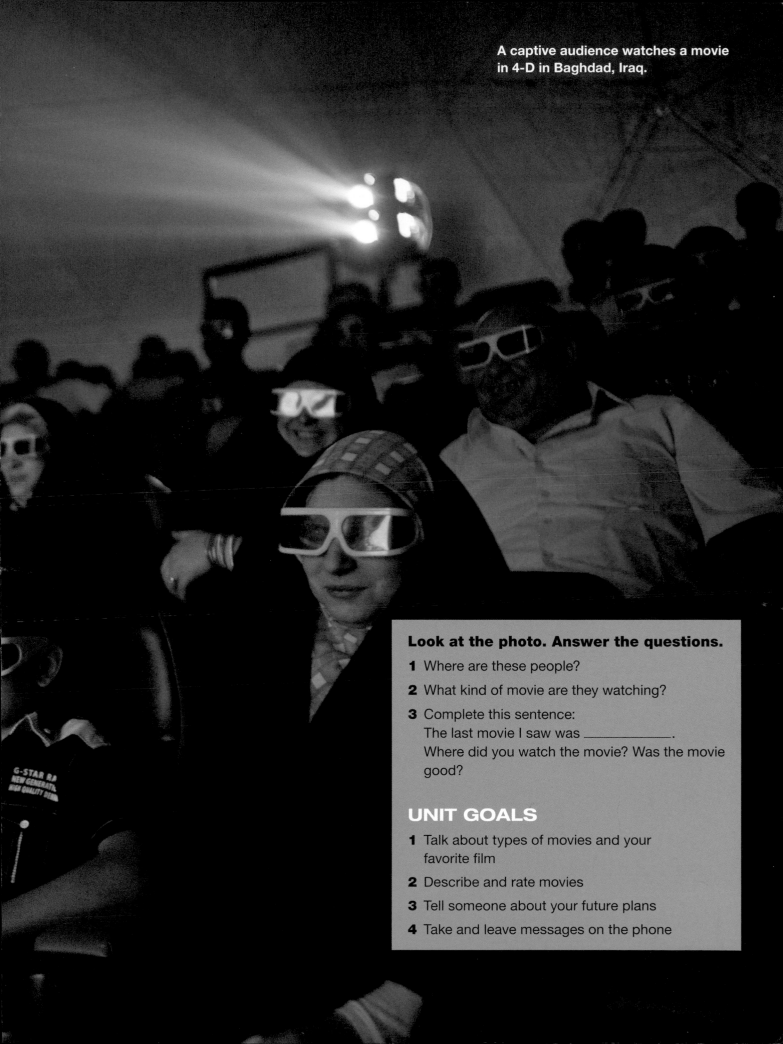

A captive audience watches a movie in 4-D in Baghdad, Iraq.

Look at the photo. Answer the questions.

1 Where are these people?

2 What kind of movie are they watching?

3 Complete this sentence:
   The last movie I saw was _____.
   Where did you watch the movie? Was the movie good?

UNIT GOALS

1 Talk about types of movies and your favorite film

2 Describe and rate movies

3 Tell someone about your future plans

4 Take and leave messages on the phone

1 **VIDEO** Spider-Man in Real Life

A Look at the photo. Do you know this character? What does he do?

B ▶ A group of people are creating a Spider-Man movie scene in real life. They are on top of a tall building in New York City.

1. Read the sentences below. Put the events in order from 1–6.

2. Watch the video and check your answers.

___ People on the street see Spider-Man.   ___ Spider-Man and the woman fly away together.

___ Spider-Man jumps off the building.   ___ Spider-Man fights the bad guy.

___ The woman thanks Spider-Man.   ___ A woman needs help.

C ▶ Read the sentences. Then watch again and circle the best answer(s). Sometimes more than one answer is possible.

1. When the people on the street see the woman, they are excited / happy / worried.

2. When Spider-Man jumps off the building, the people on the street are shocked / scared / happy.

3. When Spider-Man flies away, the people on the street are worried / happy / confused.

D 🔁 Do you know any Spider-Man movies? Do you like them? Why or why not? Tell a partner.

2 VOCABULARY

A 🔁 Talk with a partner. Answer the questions.

1. Look at the movie posters. Practice saying each type of movie. What is your favorite kind of movie? Why?

2. Read about each one. Which one do you want to see? Why?

3. Which kinds of movies **make you** laugh? cry? think? scream?

4. Do you prefer a movie with a happy ending? Why or why not?

musical / drama
Four young men come together and create a singing group…

romantic comedy
At first, Rosie and Alex were friends…

action movie
James Bond fights the bad guys…

science fiction thriller
The Robinson family is in outer space and needs to get home…

horror film
A teenager has a strange new neighbor…

classic / old movie
A young woman living in New York meets a writer in her building and…

3 LISTENING

A 🔊 **Pronunciation: Syllable stress.** Say the words. Then listen and repeat. Which syllable is stressed in each one? Underline it. **CD 2 Track 37**

romantic   comedy   <u>docu</u>mentary   musical

B 🔄 **Make predictions.** The words on the left describe movies. What do you think they mean? Discuss with a partner.

C 1. tearjerker
E 2. chick flick
   3. blockbuster
   4. indie

    a. a successful movie that costs a lot to make
    b. a less famous movie that costs less to make
    c. a movie that makes you cry
    d. a scary movie that is not good for children
    e. a romantic movie that is popular with women

C 🔊 **Check predictions.** Listen to a man and woman discuss movies. Match the words above to their definitions. One definition is extra. **CD 2 Track 38**

D 🔊 **Listen for details.** Listen again. How do the man and woman talk about likes and dislikes? Complete the sentences. **CD 2 Track 38**

1. "I'm _not into_ movies about love and romance."
2. "I thought you were _crazy about_ action movies!"
3. "Sorry, but I'm _a big fan of_ horror films either."

Word Bank
Talking about likes and dislikes
(not) crazy about   *(not) a big fan of*   *(not) into*

E 🔄 Complete the chart with one example of each type of movie. Then compare your list with a partner's. Tell your partner about one of the movies from your list.

tearjerker	
chick flick	
blockbuster	
indie	*It's not expensive movies!*

At film festivals, like Sundance, reviewers and fans have the chance to see many movies in one place.

4 SPEAKING

A 🔊 Listen to the conversation. Take a phone message for Michael. Complete the information in the box. **CD 2 Track 39**

PAM: Hello?

SILVIO: Hi. Is Michael there, please?

PAM: Who's calling?

SILVIO: This is Silvio, a friend from school.

PAM: OK. Hang on a minute.

SILVIO: Thanks.

PAM: Hello? Sorry. Michael's not here.
Can I take a message?

SILVIO: Yeah. We're going to a movie tonight.
I have an extra ticket for Michael.

PAM: OK. What time does it start?

SILVIO: In a half hour from now—at 8:00.

PAM: All right. I'll give him the message.

SILVIO: Thanks a lot.

B 🔄 Practice the conversation with a partner.

SPEAKING STRATEGY

C Think of a movie that you want to see with a friend. Then answer the questions to complete the chart.

What is the name of the movie?	Time	Place	What is your friend's name?

D 🔄 With your partner, play one of these roles in a phone conversation. Use the Useful Expressions to help you.

Student A: You call your friend to invite him or her to a movie. Your friend isn't home. Leave a message with a family member.

Student B: Answer the phone. Take a message. Fill out the note on the right.

E 🔄 Switch roles and practice again.

While You Were Out

Time of Call: _____
_____ called.
Movie is at _____. He has
_____ for you.

Useful Expressions

Taking and leaving a message

Hello? Is Michael there?

   Who's calling, please?

This is Silvio.

   OK. Hang on a minute.

   Sorry. Michael's not home yet / not here. Can I take a message?

While You Were Out

Time of Call: _____

Name of Caller: _____

Message: _____

_____

5 GRAMMAR

A Turn to page 216. Complete the exercise. Then do **B–D** below.

The Present Continuous as Future			
Subject + be	**Verb + ing**		**Future time expressions**
We're	seeing	a movie	today / tonight / tomorrow. in an hour. this weekend.
They're	making		next year.

B Complete the time expressions with a word from the box. One item does not need a word.

> in   the   this / next

1. _The_ day after tomorrow
2. _Next_ month
3. _This_ tonight
4. _In_ a few days

C 🎭 Work with a partner. Four of the sentences below correctly use the present continuous tense to talk about future plans, but two sentences do not. Cross out the two incorrect sentences.

1. We're seeing a movie later today.
2. I'm meeting them in front of the theater at 2:00.
3. We're having a lot of snow next week.
4. They're watching the Oscars tonight.
5. You need to rest or you're getting sick.
6. We're going out of town this weekend.

> ℹ️ Events that you <u>can</u> plan: a vacation, meeting friends on the weekend
> Events that you <u>cannot</u> plan: the weather, illness
> Do not use the present continuous as future for events that you <u>cannot</u> plan.

D 🎭 Look at the sentences you didn't cross out in **C**. Work with a partner to make a short conversation using at least three of the sentences.

People lining up outside of the Oscars

The Oscars are a movie awards show in the US. Go online to find out which movie won "Best Picture" last year. What country was the "Best Foreign Film" from?

6 COMMUNICATION

A 👥 Work in a small group. You are going to create a poster for a new movie. Follow the steps below.

1. Write the names of two people in your movie.

   famous actor: _____   famous actress: _____

2. Choose one of the following to appear in your movie.

   a monster   a superhero   a cowboy

   an alien   a spy   your idea: _____

3. Choose a location for your movie: _____

4. What kind of movie is it? Circle one.

   action movie   horror film   sci-fi thriller

   drama   romantic comedy   other: _____

5. Finally, choose a title for your movie: _____

B 👥 Now make the poster advertising your movie. Put your group's poster on the wall.

C 👥 Walk around and look at all the posters. Which movie do you want to see? Invite two people to see the movie with you.

> *The Monster Next Door* looks really good.

> It does. I'm a big fan of scary movies. They make me scream!

> Me too. Hey, I'm seeing it tonight at 7:00. Do you want to come?

> Sorry, but I can't. I'm going to a different movie then.

A scene from a Bollywood film

1 VOCABULARY

A 🔄 The people below watched different movies recently.

1. Take turns with a partner. Read each opinion aloud.

2. Did the person like the movie? Why or why not?

> I watched *The Hunger Games*. It was very **suspenseful**. I kept thinking, "What's going to happen next?"

> I watched a Bollywood movie. It was really **entertaining**. There was a lot of singing and dancing, and it was a **sweet** love story, too. It was a lot of fun.

> You need to see *Invictus*. It's about a rugby team from South Africa. It's very **inspiring**. You feel good and you think about life, too.

> I saw a **depressing** movie last weekend. It was so sad that I stopped watching it.

> I saw a **hilarious** movie last night. The comic in it was really funny.

> I watched this **scary** zombie movie with my boyfriend. He's crazy about them, but for me, they're too **violent**. There's too much blood!

B 🔄 Now think of movies you know. Tell your partner your ideas.

Name a(n) ＿＿＿＿＿＿＿ movie.

1. suspenseful
2. hilarious
3. inspiring
4. depressing
5. entertaining
6. sweet
7. scary
8. violent

2 LISTENING

A Read the definitions in the Word Bank. Then answer the questions. Tell a partner.

1. Where do you usually see movie trailers?

   online   on TV   at the movies

2. What movie is coming out soon? Name one.

> A new *Star Wars* movie is coming out this year.

B **Listen for a speaker's opinion.** A man and woman are talking about movies. Listen and circle the correct opinion (1a–6a) below. **CD 2 Track 40**

> ### Word Bank
>
> A *movie trailer* is an ad. It shows some scenes from a movie.
>
> When a movie *comes out*, it is available to watch.

Opinion

1a. The woman likes / dislikes the *Fast Cars* movies.

2a. The man likes / dislikes the *Fast Cars* movies.

3a. The woman likes / dislikes actress Laura Swift.

4a. The man likes / dislikes Laura Swift.

5a. The woman wants / doesn't want to see Laura Swift's new movie.

6a. The man wants / doesn't want to see Laura Swift's new movie.

Reason

1b. They are good stories / violent.

2b. They are entertaining / hilarious.

3b. She is / isn't funny.

4b. She is / isn't funny.

5b. Her new movie sounds sad / hilarious.

6b. Her new movie is funny / inspiring.

C **Listen for details.** What reason does each person give? Listen again and circle the correct reason (1b–6b) in **B**. **CD 2 Track 40**

D **Listen for details.** Listen again. Circle T for *true* and F for *false.* If a sentence is false, make it true. **CD 2 Track 40**

1. *Fast Cars 4* is an action movie.   T   F

2. *Fast Cars 4* is coming out next week.   T   F

3. Laura Swift's new movie is a comedy.   T   F

4. In her new movie, Laura Swift is a rich woman in London.   T   F

E With a partner, take turns asking the questions about the two movies you heard about.

1. What kind of movie is it?

2. Do you like these kinds of movies? Why or why not?

> What kind of movie is *Fast Cars 4*?

3 READING

A **Use background knowledge.** Look at the reading. One movie is the original; the other is a *remake* (a new version of an old film). Do you know any movie remakes?

B **Make predictions.** Look at the photos. Guess the answer to the question.

What words describe the movie *Shutter*?

a. hilarious   c. inspiring

b. scary   d. suspenseful

C **Check predictions.** Read the movie descriptions. Check your answer(s) in **B**.

What information in the reading helped you confirm or change your answer(s)? Underline it.

D **Read for details.** Which movie does each sentence describe? Check *original*, *remake*, or *both*.

1. The man's name is Tun.
   ☐ original   ☐ remake

2. The man is a photographer.
   ☐ original   ☐ remake

3. There is a car accident.
   ☐ original   ☐ remake

4. They see a girl in the photos.
   ☐ original   ☐ remake

5. The story takes place in Japan.
   ☐ original   ☐ remake

6. The critics didn't like this movie.
   ☐ original   ☐ remake

E ⚯ Answer the questions with a partner.

1. Would you like to see this movie—either the original or the remake? Why or why not?

2. What movies should not be remade?

A MOVIE REMAKE

SHUTTER (original)

In this popular film from Thailand, Tun, a photographer, and his girlfriend, Jane, are driving home on a lonely country road one night. Suddenly they see a girl in the road. Jane tries to stop the car, but it's too late. She hits and kills the girl. Feeling very afraid, Tun and Jane leave the girl and quickly drive back home to Bangkok.

Jane and Tun try to return to normal life, but then strange things start happening. Tun starts to have bad neck pain. And both Jane and Tun see strange images in Tun's photographs. They look like a girl. Is it the girl on the road?

[1] A movie *critic* watches movies and gives an opinion about them.
[2] If a movie *flops*, it isn't successful.

SHUTTER (remake)

This movie is an American remake of a Thai movie with the same name. The critics[1] thought the film would flop,[2] but it did well and made over $45 million worldwide.

The main characters are Jane and her husband Ben. They move to Tokyo for Ben's new job as a photographer. One night they are in a car accident on a country road. They hit a young girl and drive into a tree. When they wake up, they look for the girl, but they can't find her. Was the girl really there?

Jane and Ben try to forget the frightening experience, but they can't. Then Ben's shoulder starts to hurt all the time. And when Ben looks at his photos, there are strange lights in them. Ben's helper, Seiko, thinks the lights look like a girl. Is it the girl on the road?

4 GRAMMAR

A Turn to page 217. Complete the exercises. Then do **B–D** below.

-ed Adjectives	-ing Adjectives
I'm **bored**. I don't like this movie.	This movie is **boring**. Let's watch something else.

B 👥 Read the conversation. Complete each sentence with the correct adjective. Then work in a group of three and practice the conversation.

A: What did you do this weekend?

B: Not much. Mostly I watched movies.

C: What did you see?

A: I saw *Midnight on the Moon*. It was good. I was surprised / surprising.

B: Really? I saw that movie, too. I was kind of bored / boring by it.

A: You're kidding. It was amazed / amazing.

B: In my opinion, it was kind of slow and depressed / depressing in places.

A: Did you see the movie, Juan?

C: Yeah, I did.

A: What did you think?

C: Well, parts of the movie were bored / boring, but mostly it was entertained / entertaining. And the ending was excited / exciting.

A: I thought so, too!

C 👥 In the same group, think of a movie you all saw. Then, on your own, use *-ed* / *-ing* adjectives to give your opinion of the movie.

A movie we all saw: _____

My opinion of the movie: _____

How I felt watching it (use an *-ed* adjective): _____

How the movie was (use an *-ing* adjective): _____

D 👥 Use the conversation in **B** and your ideas in **C** to talk about your movie.

5 WRITING

A 🗣 Read about one person's favorite movie. Answer the questions with a partner.

1. What is the writer's favorite movie?

2. What kind of movie is it? What is it about?

3. What happens in the movie?

My Favorite Movie

My favorite movie of all time is *Cinema Paradiso*. It's a classic film from the 1980s. It's about an Italian boy named Salvatore. He loves movies.

In the film, Salvatore remembers his childhood. When he was young, he watched movies at the Cinema Paradiso, a theater in his hometown. He had an old friend named Alfredo, and he loved a girl named Elena. The movie is about these people's lives. It is a very sweet and inspiring film. You should see it!

Cinema Paradiso is *set* in Palazzo Adriano, Italy. Where a movie is set is where it takes place.

B Answer the questions in **A** about your favorite movie. Write your ideas in a few words.

C Write two paragraphs about your movie. Use your notes in **B**.

- Paragraph 1: Say the name of the movie, the kind of movie it is, and what it's about.

- Paragraph 2: Explain what happens in the movie.

- In your writing, use adjectives from this lesson.

- End with a short sentence. Tell people to see the movie.

D 🔁 Exchange papers with a partner.

1. Answer the questions in **A** about your partner's movie.

2. Circle mistakes in your partner's writing. Then return the paper to him or her.

E 👥 Make corrections to your writing. Then put together a "Must-See Movies" list with all of your classmates' ideas.

6 COMMUNICATION

A Prepare a short talk about your favorite movie.

1. Practice: Use your notes from Writing to talk about it.

2. Find a short movie trailer to use in your presentation.

B 👥 Work in a group of four. Give your presentation.

When you listen, take notes. Answer the questions in Writing **A** about your partners' movies.

C 👥 Your group talked about four movies. What do you think of each one?

Use the sentences below to tell your group.

I saw _____,... I did not see _____,...

☐ and I liked it because... ☐ but now I'd like to see it.

☐ but I didn't like it because... ☐ and I don't plan to see it.

> I saw *Thor*, but I didn't like it. I'm not into movies about comic book characters.

1 STORYBOARD

A Leo and Emma are having lunch in the cafeteria. Look at the pictures and complete the conversations. More than one answer is possible for each blank.

B 🔄 Practice the conversations with a partner. Then change roles and practice again.

2 SEE IT AND SAY IT

A 🔄 Talk about the picture with a partner.

- What's happening in the scene?
- Who looks surprised? bored? excited?
- What kind of movie is it?

B 👥 Get into a group of three or four people. You are going to perform the movie scene in the picture.

1. Discuss the scene. What's happening? Why do you think it's happening?

2. Choose a person in the scene to role-play.

3. Create a short role play of six to eight sentences. Practice it with your group.

C 👥 Perform your scene for the class.

3 TIMES CHANGE

A Look at the activities in the chart. Add one more idea. Complete the chart for yourself. Check (✓) the things you can do now and the things you knew how to do five years ago.

	Me		Partner 1		Partner 2	
	Now	5 years ago	Now	5 years ago	Now	5 years ago
drive						
speak a second language						
cook simple dishes						
your idea: _____						

B 🔁 Ask two classmates about the activities. Use *can* and *know how to* in your questions.

A: Can you drive?

B: Yes, I can. I passed the test last year.

A: Did you know how to drive five years ago?

B: No, I didn't. I was too young to drive.

C 🔀 Look at the information in your chart. Which partner are you more similar to? Tell the class.

4 LISTENING

A 🔁 Look at the pictures. Do these things ever happen where you live? Tell a partner.

☐ how to survive a tornado

☐ how to survive an earthquake

☐ how to survive a house fire

B 🔊 Listen. Tom is talking to a group of students. What are they talking about? Check (✓) the correct answer above. **CD 2 Track 42**

C 🔊 What rules do you think Tom is going to say? Make predictions. Then listen to the full conversation. Check (✓) the correct answers. **CD 2 Track 43**

☐ Open the windows.

☐ Get under a desk.

☐ Go to the store for food and water.

☐ Don't stand near the windows.

☐ Go outdoors and stand in the street.

☐ Don't use matches.

D 🔁 Have you ever been in an earthquake, a fire, a tornado, or a bad storm? Tell your partner what happened.

> Two years ago, there was a big storm. It was scary. We couldn't leave the house.

5 PLANS FOR THE DAY

A You are going to make an imaginary schedule for tomorrow. Write five activities from the box on the daily planner below.

30 minutes	1 hour	1½ hours	2 hours
go grocery shopping	go to the library	clean your apartment	do your homework
get a haircut	do research on the Internet	work out at the gym	meet a friend for coffee

10:00 AM _____   3:30 PM _____

10:30 AM _____   4:00 PM _____

11:00 AM _____   4:30 PM _____

11:30 AM _____   5:00 PM _____

12:00 PM _____   5:30 PM _____

12:30 PM _____   6:00 PM _____

1:00 PM _____   6:30 PM _____

1:30 PM _____   7:00 PM _____

2:00 PM _____   7:30 PM _____

2:30 PM _____   8:00 PM _____

3:00 PM _____   8:30 PM _____

B 🔁 Think of a fun activity. Then invite your partner to join you. Agree on a good time and write the activity in your daily planner.

A: What are you doing at 2:00 tomorrow?   B: Nothing. I'm free.

B: I'm getting a haircut.   A: Great. Do you want to see a movie?

A: How about at 3:00?   B: Sure, I'd love to!

C 🔁 Think of a different fun activity and invite a new partner to join you.

LANGUAGE SUMMARIES

UNIT 1 PEOPLE

LESSON A

Vocabulary

born in
city
contact information
email address
favorites
first / last name
friends
hometown
interested in
job
languages
phone number
subject

Speaking Strategy

Introducing Yourself

A: My name is Mariana.
B: Hi, I'm Danny. (It's) Nice to meet you.
A: (It's) Nice to meet you, too.

Asking about Occupations

A: What do you do?
B: I'm a music student.

LESSON B

Vocabulary

Use *be* with…	Use *have* with…
Age	**Eye color**
young	**(dark) brown**
in his / her teens*	**blue**
	green
in his / her twenties*	**Hairstyle**
elderly (80+)	**long ↔ short**
	straight ↔ curly
Weight	**wavy**
skinny	**spiky**
thin	
slim**	**Hair color**
average weight	**black**
heavy	**(light / dark) brown**
Height	**blond**
short	**red**
average	**gray**
tall	
	Facial hair
	beard
	mustache

*teens (13–19), twenties (ages 20–29), thirties, forties, etc.
**Slim means skinny / thin, but slim has a positive meaning.

UNIT 2 BEHAVIOR

LESSON A

Vocabulary

asking
barking
helping
looking
meeting
pointing
running
saying
shouting
sitting
smiling
talking
walking
waving to

Speaking Strategy

Greeting people and asking how they are

☺ A: Hi, _____. How's it going?
B: Fine. / OK. / All right. / Pretty good. / Not bad. How about you?
A: I'm fine, thanks.

☹ A: Hi, _____. How are you doing?
B: So-so. / Not so good.
A: Really? What's wrong?
B: I'm (a little) worried. / I'm (kind of) tired. I have a big test tomorrow.

LESSON B

Vocabulary

<u>Feelings</u>
angry
bored
confused
confident
embarrassed
excited
happy
nervous / worried
relaxed
sad

<u>Gestures / Actions</u>
bow
kiss
press noses together
shake hands

LESSON A

Vocabulary

apple
(a bunch of) **bananas**
(ground) **beef**
(a loaf of) **bread**
butter
(a piece of) **cake**
(a bunch of) **carrots**
(a box of) **cereal**
cheese
chicken
coffee
chips
(a carton of) **eggs**
fish
(a bunch of) **grapes**
(a carton of) **ice cream**
(a head of) **lettuce**
milk
noodles
(orange) **juice**
rice
salad
(a can of) **soda**
soup
sugar
tea
tofu
tomato
yogurt

fresh / frozen / junk **food**

Speaking Strategy

Talking about things you need
Do we need anything?
 Yes, we do. We need soda
  and bottled water.
 Let's see… we need…
 No, we don't. We (already) have
  everything.
What else do we need?
 We still need…
 Nothing. I think we're all set.
Anything else?
 Yes, we need…
 No, that's it. We have
  everything.

LESSON B

Vocabulary

affordable ↔ **expensive**
buy ↔ **sell**
cash
credit card
debit card
full price
go shopping
mall
on sale
pay
shop (*for* something / *at*
 a place)
shop / **spend** (**money**)

UNIT 4 VACATION

LESSON A

Vocabulary

clear
cloudy
foggy
rainy
snowy
sunny
windy

raining
snowing

(partly / mostly) (cloudy / sunny)
high / low (temperature)

chilly
cold
comfortable
freezing
hot
warm

30° = thirty degrees
−5° = minus five degrees

Speaking Strategy

Giving Advice
(I think) you should take a
    sweater.
    Good idea. / OK, I will.
    Really? I don't think so. /
    Really? I'd rather not.
I don't think you should drive. /
You shouldn't drive.
    You're probably right.
    Really? I think I'll be OK.

LESSON B

Vocabulary

buy a plane ticket
check in to ↔ check out of
    (a hotel)
get a passport
go on vacation / go on a trip
go sightseeing
pack ↔ **unpack** (a suitcase)
post photos online
take photos

UNIT 5 HEROES

LESSON A

Vocabulary

activist
ambassador
author
director
doctor
educator
explorer
founder
instructor
journalist
leader
musician
physician
politician
researcher
scientist
speaker
teacher
traveler
writer

brave
documentary

Speaking Strategy

Agreeing or disagreeing with an opinion

I think *Man on Wire* is a good movie.
  I think so, too.
  I agree.
  Yeah, you're right.

  Really? I don't think so.
  Sorry, but I disagree.
  I don't really agree.

What do you like about it?
Why do you say that?

LESSON B

Vocabulary

admire / look up to (someone)
generous
hardworking
kind
look for (something or someone)
role model / hero
smart / intelligent
work as (a doctor / scientist)

cancer
die / died
invent / invented
tool

UNIT 6 THE MIND

LESSON A

Vocabulary

bring back memories
can (sing) **from memory**
forget / remember (to do my
    homework / my house key)
forget / remember (+ noun)
good at remembering
I'll never forget the day...
**have a(n) (excellent / sharp /
    good / bad / poor) memory**
a (**happy / good / sad / painful**)
    memory

Speaking Strategy

**Expressing degrees
    of certainty**
Are they in your backpack?
    Yes, they are. / No, they aren't.
    (very certain)
    I think so. / I don't think so.
    (less certain)
    Maybe. I'm not sure. (not very
    certain)
    I have no idea. (don't know)

LESSON B

Vocabulary

(be) asleep ↔ (be) awake
fall asleep ↔ wake up
go to bed ↔ stay up (late)
get up ↔ stay in bed

dream
nightmare

UNIT 7 CITY LIFE

LESSON A

Vocabulary

ATM / cash machine
bookstore
bus station
coffee shop / cafe
copy shop
department store
gas station
grocery store / supermarket
hair salon
health club / gym
nail salon
newsstand / kiosk
nightclub
police station
taxi stand
train station

neighborhood

Speaking Strategy

**Asking for and giving
    directions**
Asking about a place in general:
Excuse me. Is there a (gas
    station) near here?
Yes. Go one block. There's one
    on the corner of (Court Street
    and First Avenue).

Asking about a specific place:
Excuse me. Where's the (Bridge
    Theater)?
It's on (Jay Street).
Go straight and turn right (on Jay
Street).
It's in the middle of the block.

LESSON B

Vocabulary

a lot of ↔ a little **pollution** (*n.*)
very ↔ not very **polluted** (*adj.*)
heavy ↔ light **traffic**
stuck in traffic
population
(public) transportation
rush hour

LESSON A

Vocabulary

play...
badminton
baseball
basketball
hockey
ping pong
soccer
tennis
volleyball

cards
darts
golf
rugby

do...
judo
pilates
yoga

gymnastics
crafts
kickboxing
puzzles

go...
bowling
jogging
skiing
surfing
swimming

camping
climbing
fishing
golfing

Speaking Strategy

Inviting with *Do you want*
Do you want to come?
  [*want* + *to* + verb]
  Sure, I'd love to!
  Sorry, I can't. I'm busy.
  Um, no thanks. I'm not
    good at…

Offering with *Do you want*
Do you want some ice cream?
  [*want* + noun]
  Yes, please. / Yes, thanks.
  No, thank you. / No, thanks.
    I'm fine.

LESSON B

Vocabulary

ambitious ↔ **laid-back** / relaxed
bright / intelligent
careful ↔ **careless**
competitive
creative
generous ↔ **selfish**
impulsive ↔ **careful**
organized ↔ **messy**
patient ↔ impatient
private
shy
talkative ↔ **reserved**
workaholic

UNIT 9 CHANGE

LESSON A

Vocabulary

**be in bad shape / be out
  of shape**
be in good shape
find / get a (new) job
gain weight ↔ lose weight
lose a job
make / earn (more / less) money
start exercising
stop / quit smoking

(New Year's) resolution
(good, bad) habit
(good, bad) quality

Speaking Strategy

**Making and responding
  to requests**
Can / Could I borrow your phone?
Can / Could you lend me your
  phone?

Positive responses
Sure. No problem.
Certainly.

Negative response
I'm sorry, but… (+ reason).

LESSON B

Vocabulary

apply for (a job)
become (something)
get ready (to do something)
goal
it takes time
prepare
relax
stop working
take it easy
take (time) **off**

UNIT 10 HEALTH

LESSON A

Vocabulary

arm
back
chest
foot
hand
head
   ear
   eye
   face
   nose
   mouth
leg
neck
shoulder
stomach

broad ↔ narrow shoulders
long ↔ short arms / legs
big / large ↔ little / small (eyes /
nose)
muscular (body)

backache
skin
fever
headache
sore throat
stomachache
temperature

Speaking Strategy

Talking about health problems
What's wrong? / What's the
  matter?
  I don't feel well.
  I'm sick.
  I have a / an (fever)
  My (leg) hurts

LESSON B

Vocabulary

be full of ↔ be low on (energy)

deal with (stress / a problem)
have time (to do something)
make a schedule

reduce (stress)
stressed ↔ relaxed
stressful ↔ relaxing
take time (to do something)

be under pressure
take a break
wait until the last minute

UNIT 11 ACHIEVEMENT

LESSON A

Vocabulary

ability
able
have a (natural) **ability**
  (to do something)

succeed
success
successful

talent
talented

post videos
get hits

audition
contest
talent show

Speaking Strategy

Compliments and follow-up questions

Compliments about things
Nice haircut!
  Where did you get it done?
Cool glasses!
  Were they expensive?
That's an interesting story! That's amazing!
  When did it happen? / What happened next?
I like your jacket a lot.
  Is it new?
What a great painting?
  How long did it take you to finish it?

Compliments about abilities
You can speak English really well!
  Where did you study?

LESSON B

Vocabulary

adventurous ↔ careful
afraid (to do something) /
  (of something) ↔ brave
(a) **challenge** (*n.*)
challenging (*adj.*)
curious (about something or
  someone) ↔ uninterested
dangerous / risky ↔ safe
frightening
give up ↔ continue
take a chance / take chances
  (*plural*) ↔ play it safe

UNIT 12 AT THE MOVIES

LESSON A

Vocabulary

action movie
blockbuster
chick flick
classic / old movie
documentary
drama
horror film
indie
musical
romantic comedy
science fiction (sci-fi) thriller
tearjerker

make you (laugh / cry / think /
scream)

(not) a (big) fan of (something)
(not) crazy about (something)
(not) into (something)

Speaking Strategy

Taking and leaving a message
Hello? Is Michael there?
  Who's calling, please?
This is Silvio.
  OK. Hang on a minute.
  Sorry. Michael's not home yet /
    not here. Can I take a
    message?

LESSON B

Vocabulary

depressing
entertaining
hilarious
inspiring
scary
suspenseful
sweet
violent
go / **see** / **watch** a movie

UNIT **1** PEOPLE

LESSON A

Review of the Simple Present Tense					
Affirmative statements			**Negative statements**		
I / You / We / They	speak	English.	I / You / We / They	don't	speak	English.
He / She / It	speaks		He / She / It	doesn't		

Yes / No questions with *be*				Short answers	
Is	she	a	student?	Yes, she **is**.	No, she**'s** not.* / No, she **isn't**.
Are	you			Yes, I **am**.	No, I**'m** not.
	they		students?	Yes, they **are**.	No, they**'re** not.* / No, they **aren't**.

*In spoken English, this negative form is more common.

Yes / No questions with other verbs				Short answers	
Do	you	speak	English?	Yes, I **do**.	No, I **don't**.
Does	she			Yes, she **does**.	No, she **doesn't**.

Wh- questions				Short answers
Where	do	you	live?	I live in Buenos Aires.
	does	he		He still lives in his hometown.
What	do	you	do?	I'm a student.
	does	she		She's a doctor.

A Complete the questions and answers. Then match each question to an appropriate answer.

1. _Do_ you live alone?
2. _What_ _do_ you do for fun?
3. _Are_ you a good student?
4. _Who_ _do_ you live with?
5. _Are_ you a teacher?
6. _What_ is your part-time job?

a. No, _I'm_ _not_. I'm a student.
b. My mother and father.
c. Yes, _I_ _am_. I get good grades.
d. I'm in a band.
e. I'm an office clerk.
f. No, I _don't_. I live with my family.

LESSON B

Describing Appearance			
Subject	*be / have*	Adjective	Noun
He	**is**	tall.	
		average	height / weight.
		young / in his teens.	
	has	blue	eyes.
		short, black	hair.

Use *be* to describe a person's height, weight, and age.

Use *have* to describe a person's eye color, hairstyle and color, and facial hair.

*The exceptions: He **is** bald. (He has no hair on his head.)

He **is** clean-shaven. (He has no hair on his face.)

When using two or more adjectives, the words usually follow this pattern:

length / size—style—color

He has **short, curly, red** hair.   She has **big blue** eyes.

A Complete the sentences with the correct form of *be* or *have*.

1. Tanya's dad *have* average height.

2. Ricardo and his sister __*have*__ wavy hair.

3. My grandmother __*be*__ in her eighties. She __*have*__ elderly.

4. I __*have*__ green eyes.

5. Max and Charlie are brothers. Max __*be*__ a beard and mustache.
   Charlie _____ clean-shaven. They both _____ blond hair.

6. Damon _____ heavy. He weighs 150 kilos.

B Look at the photo and make sentences about the woman.
Describe her appearance.

Name: Lupita Nyong'o

Job: Actress

Nationality: Kenyan, Mexican

Hair: She _____ hair.

Eyes: She _____ eyes.

Age: She _____ in

her _____ .

Weight: She _____ .

C  Tell a partner about the woman in **B**.

LESSON A

Review of the Present Continuous Tense			
Affirmative and negative statements			
I	am		
He / She / It	is	(not)	going.
You / We / They	are		

Contractions

I am → I'm
she is → she's
they are → they're

Spelling Rules

work → working
smile → smiling
sit → sitting

Yes / No questions			**Short answers**	
Is	she		Yes, she is.	No, she's not.* / No, she isn't.
Are	you	smiling?	Yes, I am.	No, I'm not.
	they		Yes, they are.	No, they're not.* / No, they aren't.

*In spoken English, this negative form is more common.

Wh- questions			**Answers**
Where	are	you	(I'm sitting) in the front row.
	is	he	sitting?	(He's sitting) over there.

A Use the words in parentheses to make questions and statements in the present continuous. Use the correct punctuation.

1. A: _____ (the dog / bark)

   B: I think he's hungry.

2. A: _____ (you / do)

   B: _____ (watch / TV)

3. A: _____ (you / study)

   B: No, I'm not. _____ (I / take a break)

4. A: Where are Eric and Susan?

   B: _____ (come / not / today)

5. A: _____ (it / go)

   B: Not bad. How about you?

6. A: Where's Tina? _____ (she / work)

   B: Yes, she is. She finishes at 5:00.

7. A: _____ (we / win / the game)

   B: _____ (we / no)

LESSON B

Object Pronouns			
Subject	**Verb**	**Object**	In English, an object pronoun (*them*) can replace a noun (*my parents*).
Leo	knows	my parents. **them**.	
I love my parents. My parents love **me**. You need help. I can help **you**.* He / She knows Jon. Jon knows **him** / **her**. It is expensive. I can't buy **it**. We are having a party. Please join **us**. They are popular. Everyone likes **them**.			Subject pronouns come before a verb: I *love* my parents. **Object pronouns** come after... a verb: My parents *love* **me**. a preposition: Jon is angry *at* **her**.

*For both singular and plural *you*

A Complete the sentences with the correct subject and object pronouns.

1. *subject*David kisses *object*his mother every day.
   _____He_____ kisses _____her_____ every day.

2. Mrs. Wang is shouting at Carlos.
   _____ is shouting at _____.

3. The dog is barking at Simone and me.
   _____ is barking at _____.

4. Simone and I are nervous about the test.
   _____ are nervous about _____.

5. In Japan, people give business cards with two hands.
   In Japan, _____ give _____ with two hands.

6. I am waving to you and Leo.
   I am waving to _____. Can you see _____?

B Read the sentences. Underline the subject. Circle the object.

1. Angie is waving to (her son).

2. Tom is smiling at Jane.

3. Carlos is worried about the test.

4. Do your parents like Indian food?

5. Peter and Cindy are talking to Bill and Anna.

6. Rick and I can meet you and Mike at 3:00.

7. The dog is barking at Taylor and me.

8. Maya is calling David on her cell phone.

C Rewrite the sentences in **B**. Use the correct subject and object pronouns.

1. *She's waving to him* _____.

2. _____.

3. _____.

4. _____.

5. _____.

6. _____.

7. _____.

8. _____.

UNIT 3 SHOPPING

LESSON A

Count Nouns		Noncount Nouns		
Singular	**Plural**			
apple	apples	beef	bread	English divides nouns into things we can count (count nouns) and things we can't (noncount nouns). Count nouns have singular and plural forms.
carrot	carrots	cereal	cheese	
tomato	tomatoes	rice	soda	

Singular and Plural Count Nouns; Noncount Nouns					
	Article	**Noun**	**Verb**		
Singular count nouns	A	banana	is	a good snack.	Use *a / an* or *the* before the noun.
	The	banana	is	in the bowl.	Use a singular form of the verb.
Plural count nouns	—	Bananas	are	good for you.	Use *the* or no article before the noun.
	The	bananas	are	on the table.	Use a plural form of the verb.
Noncount nouns	—	Bread	is	inexpensive.	Use *the* or no article before the noun.
	The	bread	is	in the bag.	Use a singular form of the verb.

Partitives: Talking about Specific Amounts							
General amount			**Specific amount**				
Please buy	some	bread.	Please buy	a	loaf	of	bread.
		lettuce.			head		lettuce.
		ice cream.			carton		eggs.
		carrots.			bunch		grapes.

a bottle of water	a glass of juice / water	a cup of coffee / soup
a can of soup / soda	a piece of cake / chocolate	a slice of bread / pie

A Read this recipe for beef stir fry. Circle the count nouns. Underline the noncount ones.

Pour some (1.) oil into (2.) a pan and heat it up.

Add (3.) some garlic, (4.) mushrooms, and (5.) carrots into the pan and cook them.

Remove the garlic and (6.) the vegetables from the pan.

Next, cook (7.) the beef.

Put (8.) the meat and (9.) vegetables together and cover with (10.) soy sauce.

Serve over (11.) rice on (12.) a dinner plate.

Don't forget to have (13.) a drink with it!

LESSON B

Yes / No Questions with *any*		Answers
Plural count nouns	Do you have **any**	friends?	Yes, I do.
Noncount nouns		money?	No, I don't.

Use *any* in *Yes / No* questions to ask about unknown amounts.

Quantifiers with Affirmative and Negative Statements			
		Quantifier	**Noun**
Plural count nouns	I have	a lot of / many some	friends.
	I don't have	a lot of / many any	
Noncount nouns	I have	a lot of some	money.
	I don't have	a lot of / much any	

Quantifiers give information about an amount of something.

You can answer a question with a short answer:

Do you have **any** friends?   Yes, I have **a lot** (of friends).

Do you have **any** money?   No, I don't have **much** (money), just two dollars.

Notice: *I don't have **any** friends / money. = I have **no** friends / money.*

A   Complete each sentence with the best answer.

1. Juan has $1,000,000. He has much / a lot of money.

2. Barry only has $2. He doesn't have any / much money.

3. This store only sells clothes. You can't buy any / many shoes here.

4. Rita has a lot of / many beautiful jewelry.

5. There aren't much / many department stores in this city. There are only two.

6. Leo has three friends. He has many / some friends.

B   🔗 Write a quantifier in each blank. Then practice the dialogs with a partner.

1. A: Do you have _____ questions about the homework?

    B: No, I don't have _____. I understand everything.

2. A: Are there _____ girls in this class?

    B: Yes, there are _____—three, I think.

3. A: Do you have _____ cash? I want a soda.

    B: Yes, but I don't have _____. I only have $1.

4. A: Is there _____ room in the closet for my suitcase?

    B: Yes, the closet is empty. There's _____ room.

UNIT 4   VACATION

LESSON A

Connecting Ideas with *but, or,* and *so*	
It's freezing in Moscow, **but** it's warm in Rio. It's cold **but** sunny in Lima today. It's a nice day **but** a little hot.	Use *but* to show an opposite idea or contrast. *But* joins words, phrases, and sentences.
We can go to the beach, **or** we can visit the zoo. Is it warm **or** chilly outside? Do you want coffee **or** tea?	Use *or* to give choices. *Or* joins words, phrases, and sentences.
It's raining, **so** we're not having a picnic today. My hometown is Seoul, **so** I know it well.	Use *so* to introduce a result. *So* joins sentences.

A   Complete the sentences with *but, or,* or *so.*

1. William can't speak French, _____ Marion can.

2. Roberto is very healthy. He doesn't drink _____ smoke.

3. It's foggy outside, _____ I don't think you need sunglasses.

4. Does the movie start at 7:00 _____ 7:30?

5. Tokyo is an exciting city, _____ it's very expensive to live in.

6. It's 32° C / 90° F out, _____ I'm wearing a T-shirt.

7. It's snowing outside, _____ Mario is wearing shorts.

8. For dinner, you can have chicken, fish, _____ beef.

B   Combine the two sentences using *but, or,* or *so.*

1. Kaz likes to travel. His girlfriend doesn't like to travel.

   Kaz likes to travel, but his girlfriend doesn't _____.

2. We can go to Martin's party. We can see a movie.

   _____.

3. John is sick. He's not coming to class today.

   _____.

4. It's a beautiful day. We're having class outside.

   _____.

5. I'm wearing my glasses. I can't see the whiteboard.

   _____.

6. Rosa wants to study at an American university. She's taking the TOEFL exam.

   _____.

LESSON B

	Possessive Adjectives	Possessive Pronouns	*belong to*
Whose passport is this?	It's **my** passport.	It's **mine**.	It **belongs to** me.
	your	**yours**.	**you**.
	her	**hers**.	**her**.
	his	**his**.	**him**.
	our	**ours**.	**us**.
	their	**theirs**.	**them**.

Whose and *who's* have the same pronunciation but different meanings.

Whose asks about the owner of something: *Whose house is that? It's mine.*

Who's is a contraction of *Who* and *is*: *Who's studying English? Maria is.*

A Write the correct possessive pronoun for the underlined words.

1. A: That's not her suitcase.

    B: No, *hers* <u>her suitcase</u> is over there.

2. A: Can I use your cell phone? <u>My cell phone</u> doesn't work.

    B: Sorry, but I forgot my cell phone at home. Use <u>Jon's phone</u>.

3. A: Is your class fun?

    B: Yes, but <u>Aya and Leo's class</u> is more interesting.

4. A: Is your hometown hot in the summer? <u>My hometown</u> is.

    B: <u>Our hometown</u> is, too.

5. A: Your birthday is in May.

    B: That's right, and <u>your birthday</u> is in March.

B Use the words in the chart to complete the conversation. Then practice the dialog with a partner.

JIM: Well, I have (1.) _____*my*_____ luggage. Where's
(2.) _____ ?

BEN: Um... let's see... oh, here's (3.) _____
suitcase. No, wait... this one isn't (4.) _____ .

JIM: (5.) _____ is it?

BEN: It says Mr. Simon Konig. It belongs to (6.) _____ .

JIM: Hey, I think that man has (7.) _____
suitcase. See? He probably thinks it's
(8.) _____ .

BEN: I'll ask him. Excuse me, does this suitcase belong
to (9.) _____ ?

SIMON: Oh, sorry. My mistake! I thought it was (10.) _____ !

UNIT 5 HEROES

LESSON A

Past Forms of *be*
am / is → **was**
am not / isn't → **wasn't**
are → **were**
aren't → **weren't**

The Simple Past Tense with *be*

Affirmative and Negative Statements

Subject	*was / were*	
I	**was / wasn't**	
You	**were / weren't**	brave.
He / She / It	**was / wasn't**	
We / You / They	**were / weren't**	

Yes / No Questions

Was / Were	Subject		Answers
Were	you		Yes, I **was**. / No, I **wasn't**.
	they	brave?	Yes, they **were**. / No, they **weren't**.
Was	she		Yes, she **was**. / No, she **wasn't**.
	I		Yes, you **were**. / No, you **weren't**.

Wh- Questions				Answers
Wh- word	*was / were*	Subject		
Where	**were**	you	yesterday?	At home.
When	**was**	he	in Iceland?	Two years ago.
Who	**was**	your teacher	last semester?	Ms. Hunter.

You can use these time expressions with the past tense of *be*: yesterday, **in** 1990, **last** semester / week, two days / years **ago**.

A Complete the conversation with a partner. Use the correct form of the verb *be* in the past tense.

TIM: Hi, Kelly. It's Tim. I called you yesterday, but you (1. not) _____ home.

KELLY: I (2.) _____ at the library. I'm writing a paper about Pierre and Marie Curie.

TIM: They (3.) _____ scientists from France, right?

KELLY: Right. Well, actually Pierre (4.) _____ French, but his wife (5. not) _____ born in France. She (6.) _____ from Poland. She (7.) _____ also the first person to win a Nobel Prize twice.

B Complete the questions on the left. Then match them with the correct answers on the right.

1. _____ Kelly at home?
2. _____ _____ Kelly?
3. _____ the Curies scientists?
4. _____ Marie Curie born in France?
5. _____ _____ Marie Curie born?
6. _____ Marie Curie the first person to win two Nobel Prizes?
7. _____ _____ Pierre Curie from?
8. _____ _____ the Curies?

a. Yes, they were.
b. No, she wasn't.
c. No, she wasn't.
d. They were scientists.
e. Yes, she was.
f. France.
g. At the library.
h. In Poland.

LESSON B

The Simple Past: Affirmative and Negative Statements		
I / You / He / She / We / They	visit**ed** **didn't** visit	Tokyo.
I / You / He / She / We / They	start**ed** **didn't** start	a company.

In the simple past tense, the verb form is the same for all persons.

In affirmative statements, add –*ed* or –*d*. See the spelling rules below.

In negative statements, use *did not* or *didn't* + the base form of the verb.

The Simple Past Tense of Regular Verbs: Spelling Rules	
mov**e** → mov**ed**	If the verb ends in *e*, add –*d*.
star**t** → start**ed**	If the verb ends with a consonant, add –*ed*.
stu**dy** → stud**ied**	If the verb ends with a consonant + *y*, change the *y* to *i* and add –*ed*.
pl**ay** → play**ed**	If the verb ends with a vowel + *y*, add –*ed*.
st**op** → stop**ped**	With one-syllable verbs that end with a consonant–vowel–consonant, double the last letter and add –*ed*.
fi**x** → fix**ed**	But do not double the last consonant if it is a *w* or *x*.
oc**cur** → occur**red**	With two-syllable verbs that end with a consonant–vowel–consonant, double the last consonant if the last syllable is stressed.
lis**ten** → listen**ed**	But do not double the last consonant if the last syllable is not stressed.

A Complete the sentences with the simple past tense of each verb. Pay attention to spelling.

1. Sanga Moses (work) _____ in a bank in the capital.

2. One day, he (visit) _____ his family.

3. He saw his sister. She (carry) _____ a lot of wood that day.

4. She (look) _____ at her brother, and she (cry) _____. She said,
   "I (not go) _____ to school today. I (walk) _____ 10 kilometers to get wood."

5. Sanga Moses (want) _____ his sister to stay in school.

6. That day, he (decide) _____ to do something. He (stop) _____ working at the bank.
   He (start) _____ Eco-Fuel Africa.

7. With a group of engineers, he (invent) _____ a new oven. It (change) _____ many
   people's lives in Uganda.

B Make sentences about things you did or didn't do yesterday. Use the verbs.

1. walk to school _____ I didn't walk to school. _____
2. text a friend _____
3. listen to a song in English _____
4. study for a test _____
5. cook dinner _____
6. watch TV _____
7. hug my mom _____
8. wash my hair _____

UNIT 6   THE MIND

LESSON A

The Simple Past: Affirmative and Negative Statements (Irregular Verbs)			
Subject	***did + not***	**Verb**	
I / You / He / She / We / They		forgot	her birthday.
	didn't	forget	

- In affirmative statements, do not add -ed to form irregular past tense verbs. See the chart below for the simple past tense form of many common irregular verbs.
- In negative statements, use *did not* or *didn't* + the base form of the verb.

Present	Past	Present	Past	Present	Past	Present	Past	Present	Past
begin	began	drink	drank	give	gave	meet	met	sing	sang
bring	brought	eat	ate	go	went	pay	paid	speak	spoke
buy	bought	fall	fell	have	had	read	read*	take	took
choose	chose	feel	felt	know	knew	run	ran	teach	taught
come	came	forget	forgot	leave	left	say	said	think	thought
do	did	get	got	make	made	see	saw	wear	wore

*Note: There is a vowel shift in the past tense pronunciation of *read*. The vowel goes from /i/ to /ɛ/.

A Complete the story with the simple past form of the verbs in parentheses. Most of the verbs are irregular. Which ones are regular?

A Scary Memory

There (1. be) _____ a fire one day when I (2. be) _____ at school. It (3. begin) _____ around lunchtime. Soon, we all (4. smell) _____ smoke. Someone (5. say) _____ in a loud voice, "Fire!" Then the fire alarm (6. ring) _____. As we (7. walk) _____ down the hallway, I (8. feel) _____ the heat from the fire. We (9. not say) _____ anything—everyone was so quiet.

The fire truck (10. come) _____ quickly. The firefighters (11. run) _____ into the building and (12. stop) _____ the fire. After 30 minutes, we (13. go) _____ back into our school. Luckily, there (14. not be) _____ much damage. I will never forget that day.

B 🔄 Take turns reading the story in **A** with a partner. Then explain the story in your own words. Can you retell it from memory?

LESSON B

The Simple Past Tense: *Yes / No* Questions				
Did	**Subject**	**Verb**		**Short answers**
Did	you he / she / it they	stay up late wake up	last night?	Yes, I did. / No, I didn't. Yes, he did. / No, he didn't. Yes, they did. / No, they didn't.

- To ask a past tense *Yes / No* question, use *did* + subject + base form of the verb.
- Short answers are the same for both regular and irregular verbs.

The Simple Past Tense: *Wh-* Questions				
Wh- word	**did**	**Subject**	**Verb**	**Answers**
When	did	you he / she / it they	study?	(I / She / They studied) last night.
			get up?	(I / She / They got up) at 7:00.
What			happened to you?	I woke up late this morning.

A Circle the mistake in each dialog and correct it.

1. A: Did Mario stayed up late last night?

   B: Yes, he did.

2. A: Did you forget your keys?

   B: No, I didn't forgot them.

3. A: Where did Julie went on her vacation?

   B: She went to Mexico.

4. A: What did happen to Yu and Amy?

   B: They slept late and missed the bus.

B Complete the dialogs with a past tense *Yes / No* or *Wh-* question or short answer.

1. A: _when did you ___ to sleep_ last night?

   B: I went to bed at 10:00.

2. A: _did you sleep_ well?

   B: No, I didn't sleep well. I had nightmares.

3. A: _Did you drink coffee_ before bed?

   B: No, _I didn't_. I never drink coffee before bed.

4. A: Did you eat before bed?

   B: Yes, _I did_.

5. A: _What did you_ last night?

   B: I ate a piece of cake. Maybe that caused the bad dreams. _dream_

6. A: _what did you_ about?

   B: I dreamt about zombies.

C 🔁 Practice the conversations in **B** with a partner.

UNIT **7** CITY LIFE

LESSON A

Prepositions of Place: *at, on,* and *in*	
A: Where are you? B: I'm **at** school. I'm **on** the second floor, **in** my classroom.	• Use *at* + building: *at the mall, at home* • Use *on* + floor: *on the top floor* • Use *in* + room: *in my office, in the kitchen*
A: Where is it? B: It's **at** 30 Grant Avenue. / It's **on** Grant Avenue.	• Use *at* + address: *at 100 Smith Street* • Use *on* + street: *on Smith Street*

A 🔁 Complete the conversation with *at, on, in,* or other prepositions of location from p. 100. Then practice it with a partner.

A: Where are you?

B: I'm still (1.) _at_ work!

A: Really? The movie starts in 25 minutes!

B: I know! Where is the theater again?

A: It's (2.) _on_ Oak Street. Let's see… it's (3.) _at_ 200 Oak Street, to be exact. The theater is (4.) _on_ the third floor.

B: OK. Got it. I'm catching a taxi soon.

A: Tell the driver the theater is (5.) _next_ to a police station. Let's meet (6.) _in front_ of the theater.

   And after the movie, we can go to the nightclub (7.) _straight_ from the theater.

B: OK, see you soon!

B Circle the correct words. Complete the sentences with information about yourself.

1. I'm at / on / in school every day from _8:30_ to _1:00pm_.

2. My classroom is at / on / in the _~~first~~ 3ᵗʰ_ floor.

3. There are a lot of _books_ at / on / ⓘⓝ my classroom.

4. My school is at / ⓞⓝ / in a _busy_ street.

LESSON B

Questions and Answers with *How much / How many*	
Count nouns	**Noncount nouns**
How many parks are there in your city?	**How much** pollution is there?

	Count nouns	Noncount nouns
Affirmative	(There are) **a lot / many.** 　　　**some / a few.** 　　　**two.**	(There's) **a lot.** 　　　**some / a little.** 　　　----------
Negative	There aren't **many. / Not many.** There aren't **any. / None.**	There isn't **much. / Not much.** There isn't **any. / None.**

How many is used with count nouns. *How much* is used with noncount nouns.

A few means a very small number of something.

It's common to answer *How much / How many* questions with a short answer:

(*There are) a lot (of parks).*　　　(*There's) a little (pollution).*

The short answers in the negative are *Not many, Not much,* and *None.*

A Circle the best word to complete each sentence.

1. There isn't many / any traffic on the road at the moment.

2. Yesterday, there was a lot of smog, but today, there's only a little / a few.

3. How many / much people live in your neighborhood?

4. A: How many / much rain does this city get in the winter?

   B: It gets a lot / much.

B Complete the dialogs with the words in **bold** in the chart.

1. A: How _____ bookstores are there in this city?

   B: Not _____. Most people buy books online now.

2. A: How _____ traffic is there at 8:30 in the morning?

   B: There's _____. You can be stuck in traffic for an hour or more.

3. A: How _____ friends do you have?

   B: _____. I just moved here. I only know one or two people.

4. A: How _____ homework do we have tonight?

   B: _____. The teacher didn't give us any.

5. A: Do you have _____ free time on the weekend?

   B: I have _____, about an hour or two.

6. A: How _____ Thai restaurants are there in your city?

   B: There are _____. We don't even have one Thai restaurant.

C 🔁 Now ask and answer the questions in **B** with a partner. Use your own answers.

UNIT 8 ALL ABOUT YOU

LESSON A

Verb + Infinitive	
I **love** <u>to play</u> volleyball. I **forgot** <u>to explain</u> the rules. Can you **learn** <u>to surf</u> in one summer?	The infinitive is *to* + the base form of the verb. It can follow these common verbs: *forget, hate, learn, like, love, need, decide, plan, prepare,* and *want*.

Verb + Noun	
I **like** <u>most sports</u>. I**'m planning** <u>a big trip</u>. We **prepared** <u>dinner</u> for everyone.	All the verbs above can also be followed by a noun or noun phrase.

A Use the verb in parentheses to complete each sentence with the verb + *to* or the verb alone. (Some of the verbs may be in the simple past tense.)

1. I (want) _____ go camping next weekend.

2. Don't (forget) _____ explain the rules.

3. Do you (hate) _____ gym class?

4. I have a silver medal, and now I (want) _____ a gold one.

5. You (need) _____ stretch before you do pilates.

6. I can't go swimming because I (forget) _____ my swimsuit.

7. I'm serious about ping pong. I (hate) _____ lose.

8. I (learn) _____ a new game. Do you want me to show you?

LESSON B

How often...? Frequency Expressions			
How often do you see your best friend?	(I see her)	**every**	day / Monday / week / month / summer.
		once **twice** **three times** **several times**	a day / a week / a month / a year.
		all the time. (= very often) *I see her all the time.* **once in a while**. (= sometimes) *I see her once in a while.* **hardly ever.*** (= almost never) *I hardly ever see her.* **never**. (= not ever)* *I never see her.*	

How often asks about the frequency of an event.

*Frequency expressions usually come at the end of a sentence, but it's more common for *hardly ever* and *never* to come before the verb: "*I **hardly ever** <u>see</u> her.*" "*I **never** <u>see</u> my best friend.*"

To say something never happens, you can also say: *Never.*

A 🎧 Find the mistake in each dialog and correct it. Then practice the dialogs with a partner.

1. A: How often you play tennis?

   B: Every Sunday.

2. A: How often do you wash your hair?

   B: Once a week, on Monday and Friday.

3. A: Is the bus usually on time?

   B: No, it's all the time late.

4. A: How often does Maria see her brother?

   B: Hardly ever she sees him. He works in the UK.

B Look at Ricardo's weekly schedule. Answer the questions with a word or phrase in **bold** in the chart.

Monday	Tuesday	Wednesday	Thursday	Friday	Saturday	Sunday
Class: 9–12 Work: 1–4	Work: 10–2	Class: 9–12 Work: 1–4	Work: 10–2	Class: 9–12 Work: 1–4	Study group: 10–12 Work: 1–4	Work: 3–6

How often does Ricardo...

1. have class?

2. work?

3. work from 10 to 2?

4. work from 1 to 4?

5. meet with his study group?

Answer

1a. _____once_____ a week.

1b. _____on_____ Monday, Wednesday, and Friday.

2a. _____ day.

2b. _____ time.

3a. _____ a week.

3b. _____ Tuesday and Thursday.

4a. _____ a week.

4b. _____ Monday, Wednesday, Friday, and Saturday.

5a. _____.

5b. _____.

UNIT **9** CHANGE

LESSON A

Like to Versus Would like to						
Do		**like**	**Infinitive**			
	I				in the Outback.	
Do	you	**like**	to spend	time	there?	

Use *like* + the infinitive form to talk about the present.

		Would	**like**	**Infinitive**		
I		**would***	**like**	to spend	time	in the Outback.
	Would	you				there?

*It's common to use the contracted form: *I'd like to spend time in the Outback.*

Use *would like* + the infinitive form to talk about a future hope or desire.

Contractions

I'd = I would
you'd = you would
he'd = he would
she'd = she would
we'd = we would
they'd = they would

A ⟳ Use the words in the box to complete the conversations. Then practice them with a partner.

I like	do you like	I'd like
I don't like	do you like	I'd like
I'd like	would you like	you'd like

A: This menu looks interesting. (1.) _____ to try something new, but I can't decide.

B: Well, what kind of food (2.) _____?

A: Let's see… (3.) _____ anything too strange… and (4.) _____ spicy food.

B: Then I think (5.) _____ the red curry. It's really spicy… and very delicious!

A: It sounds good. I think (6.) _____ that.

A: What changes (7.) _____ to make in the new year?

B: Well, for one, (8.) _____ to lose some weight. I'm out of shape.

A: I see… and, (9.) _____ to exercise?

B: Yes, I do, actually. I started exercising last month.

A: Come with me to the gym tomorrow, then. We can work out together.

LESSON B

The Future with *be going to*						
Subject	***be***	**(not)**	***going to***	**Base form**		**Future time expression**
I	**am**	(not)	**going to**	start	college	tomorrow.
You	**are**					this fall.
He / She	**is**					in August.
We / You / They	**are**					next week / month / year.
						after graduation.

Use *be going to* to talk about future plans.

You can also use it to make predictions: *She's going to be a great doctor.*

When the subject is a pronoun, it's common to use a contraction with *be*: *I'm going to start college…*

With a noun + *be going to*, we often say the contraction: *My <u>sister's</u> going to take some time off.*

Don't use the contraction in formal writing.

Yes / No questions						Short answers	
Is	she	**going to**	start	college	this fall?	Yes, she is.	No, she's not. / No, she isn't.
Are	you					Yes, I am.	No, I'm not.
	they					Yes, they are.	No, they're not. / No they aren't.

Wh- questions						Answers
When	is	he	**going to**	start	college?	(He's / I'm going to start college) in August.
	are	you				

A Complete the sentences about a student's summer plans with the correct form of *be going to*.

I (1. visit) _____ Europe after graduation. My brother (2. stay) _____

home. He (3. not travel) _____ anywhere. He (4. take) _____ it easy.

My parents (5. take) _____ a week off from work. They (6. meet) _____

me in Paris. We (7. not return) _____ home until September 5.

B Complete the conversation using questions and answers with *be going to*.

JO: So, (1. when / you / leave) _____ for Europe?

NEIL: Next month.

JO: (2. you / go) _____ alone?

NEIL: No, (3. my roommate / come) _____ with me.

JO: (4. Where / you / start) _____ your trip?

NEIL: First, (5. we / fly) _____ to London.
Then (6. I / visit) _____ two more cities alone.

JO: (7. your / parents / visit) _____ you in Europe?

NEIL: Yes, (8. they / meet) _____ me in Paris.

C 🔁 In your notebook, write three *be going to* questions to ask about your partner's summer plans. Then interview your partner.

UNIT **10** HEALTH

LESSON A

Affirmative and Negative Forms of the Imperative			
Don't	**Base form**		
	Stay	calm.	Use the imperative to give advice, instructions, directions, and orders.
Don't	panic.		
	Go	to the airport.	
Don't	leave	without your passport.	Add *please* to make orders and requests more polite: *Please don't smoke here. Move outside, please.*
	Take	two aspirin daily.	
Don't	forget	to take your medicine.	

A ⚡ Complete each item with the correct answer. Then compare your answers with a partner.

1. I feel sick. Please take _____ .

    a. me to the doctor   b. some medicine

2. We're leaving for the airport. Don't _____ your passport.

    a. bring   b. forget

3. Shh! _____ quiet. _____ any noise.

    a. Don't be; Make   b. Be; Don't make

4. Does your eye hurt? Don't _____!

    a. rub it   b. put in eye drops

5. _____ the instructions again, please. I couldn't hear you the first time.

    a. Read   b. Don't read

6. It says, "Be careful! _____ this medicine on an empty stomach."

    a. Bring   b. Don't take

LESSON B

When Clauses	
When clause	**Result clause**
When(ever) I drink coffee,	I can't sleep.
Result clause	**When clause**
I can't sleep	when(ever) I drink coffee.

These sentences talk about things that are usually true: When *X* happens, *Y* is the result.

The present tense is used in the *when* clause and the result clause.

The result clause can come first or second in a sentence. When it comes first, there is no comma between the result clause and the *when* clause.

A Match a *when* clause on the left with a result clause on the right to make sentences.

1. When I feel stressed,   a. people are usually nice to you.

2. When we argue,   b. I get hungry by 10:00.

3. When I sleep well,   c. my mom usually apologizes first.

4. When I don't eat breakfast,   d. I exercise.

5. When you're kind,   e. I'm late for class.

6. When I miss the bus,   f. I have a lot of energy.

B 🔄 Rewrite the sentences in **A** so that the result comes first. Then tell your partner which sentences are true for you. Explain your answers.

1. <u>I exercise when I feel stressed</u>   .

2. _____ .

3. _____ .

4. _____ .

5. _____ .

6. _____ .

C 🔄 Compare your answers in **B** with a different partner.

> I exercise when I feel stressed.

> Really? I don't.

UNIT **11** ACHIEVEMENT

LESSON A

<table>
<tr><td colspan="4">Using can for Ability</td></tr>
<tr><td>Subject</td><td>Modal verb</td><td>Base form</td><td></td></tr>
<tr><td>I / You</td><td rowspan="3">can / can't
could / couldn't</td><td rowspan="3">sing</td><td rowspan="3">well.</td></tr>
<tr><td>He / She / It</td></tr>
<tr><td>We / You / They</td></tr>
<tr><td></td><td>Modal verb</td><td>Base form</td><td></td></tr>
<tr><td></td><td>Can you</td><td>sing</td><td>well?</td></tr>
</table>

Use *can* to talk about abilities you learn: *I can ride a bicycle.*

The modal verb *can* has the same form for all persons: *I can, she can,* etc.

Questions and the negative are formed without *do.*

You can also use *know how to* to talk about learned abilities but not for non-learned abilities: *I can't see without my glasses. ~~I don't know how to see without my glasses.~~*

> ℹ️ Do not use *could* to talk about past abilities if it's a one-time achievement. Use *was able to* instead: ~~I could win first place in the contest.~~ *I was able to win first place in the contest.*

A Read about Phiona Mutesi, a young chess champion from Uganda. Complete her story with *can, can't, could, couldn't,* or *be able to* (where necessary).

Phiona Mutesi loved to study, but her mother (1.) _____ pay Phiona's school fees. Phiona stopped going to school.

She was unhappy, but then she discovered the game of chess. She (2.) _____ learn the rules of the game in one day!

She had a natural ability and (3.) _____ soon beat other players.

In two years, she (4.) _____ win the junior girls Ugandan national championship.

Nowadays, you (5.) _____ read about Phiona in the news. She travels and plays chess all over the world.

Phiona's story inspires us. You (6.) _____ succeed when you practice and work hard.

LESSON B

Connecting Ideas with *because*	
Main clause	**Reason clause**
He likes to fly	**because** it's exciting.
Reason clause	**Main clause**
Because it's exciting,	he likes to fly.

Because can join two clauses together. A clause has a subject and a verb.

Because answers the question *why*. It gives a reason for an action: *Why does he like to fly? (He likes to fly) because it's exciting.*

In conversation, people often give the reason only *(Because it's exciting.)*. Don't do this in formal writing.

In writing, when the reason comes first, put a comma before the main clause.

Connecting Ideas with *so*	
Main clause	**Result clause**
The weather was bad,	**so** he didn't fly.

So can join two clauses together.

So gives a result: *The weather was bad.* The result: *He didn't fly.*

In writing, use a comma before *so* unless the two clauses are very short.

A Complete each sentence with *because* or *so*. If you use *so*, remember to add a comma to the sentence.

1. Many risk-takers are successful _____ they take chances.

2. My mom is afraid to fly _____ she always drives places.

3. Smoking is dangerous _____ Jon quit.

4. Bruno is nervous _____ he has a job interview.

5. I'm afraid to go to the dentist _____ I never go.

6. Elena did well on the exam _____ she studied hard.

7. They started their own business _____ they don't work for others.

8. I didn't understand a word _____ I used my dictionary.

9. Everyone knows that video _____ it was popular last month.

10. Anh is disinterested in the movie _____ he thinks it is boring.

B Rewrite the five *because* sentences from **A** so the word *because* starts the sentence.

1. _____.
2. _____.
3. _____.
4. _____.
5. _____.

C Unscramble the words to make sentences. Use commas if necessary.

1. don't / I / go rock climbing / it's / dangerous / because

_____.

2. cold / was / it / didn't / go to the beach / we / so

_____.

3. cold / was / it / didn't / go to the beach / we / because

_____.

4. the exam / I / failed / it / have to / retake / so / I

_____.

UNIT **12**   **AT THE MOVIES**

LESSON A

The Present Continuous as Future		
Subject + *be*	**Verb + *ing***	**Future time expression**
We're	seeing	a movie	today / tonight / tomorrow. in an hour. this weekend.
They're	making		next year.

You can use the present continuous tense (often with a future time expression) to talk about future plans.

Use the present continuous only when a plan exists:

Here's the plan: We're meeting downtown and then driving to the theater in my car.

Do not use the present continuous to make predictions. Use *going to* instead:

~~He's passing the test tomorrow.~~ He's going to pass the test tomorrow.

A Complete the conversation. Use the present continuous form of the verbs in parentheses and complete the time expression with the words in the box.

> Verbs that are related to movement and travel (like *go, come, take, fly, travel, visit, leave, arrive,* and *get*) are commonly used in the present continuous when expressing future time.

in	next	this	tomorrow

A: I'm really looking forward to summer vacation (1.) ____this____ year.

B: Why is that?

A: Because (2. I / go) _____ to Tanzania, in Africa. (3. we / leave)
_____ (4.) _____ morning! I'm so excited!

B: Wow! How (5. you / get) _____ there?

A: (6. we / fly) _____ with Global Airways from New York City. And
(7. we / change) _____ planes in Dubai before arriving in Dar es Salaam.

B: Do you already have a plan for the trip?

A: Yes, (8. we / visit) _____ Zanzibar for a few days and then (9. climb)
_____ Mount Kilimanjaro.

B: Great! How long is the trip?

A: (10. I / stay) _____ for two weeks, so (11. I / return) _____ early
(12.) _____ month. (13. my friend / travel) _____ an extra week
in Africa. What about you? (14. you / go) _____ anywhere fun?

B: Not really. (15. I / visit) _____ my family down south. (16. I / drive)
_____ and (17. I / leave) _____ (18.) _____ a few hours.

LESSON B

-ed Adjectives	*-ing* Adjectives
1a. I'm **bored**. I don't like this movie.	**1b.** This movie is **boring**. Let's watch something else.
2a. I was **surprised** by the ending.	**2b.** The end of the movie was **surprising**.

Use *-ed* adjectives to describe a person's feelings. For example, in sentence 1a, you can say *I'm bored*, (meaning "I feel bored") but not ~~I'm boring~~.

Use *-ing* adjectives to describe a situation, an activity, or person that makes you feel a certain way: *That movie was boring. My math teacher is very inspiring.*

Here are some common *-ed* / *-ing* adjectives. Review their meanings with your instructor and classmates.

amazed / amazing	embarrassed / embarrassing	interested / interesting
bored / boring	entertained / entertaining	relaxed / relaxing
confused / confusing	excited / exciting	shocked / shocking
depressed / depressing	frightened / frightening	surprised / surprising
disappointed / disappointing	inspired / inspiring	terrified / terrifying

A Complete the movie review. Circle the correct words. Did Paula like the movie?

Actor Sean Clarkson is in the new sci-fi thriller *Midnight on the Moon*. Overall, I was very disappointed / disappointing with this film. Some scenes in the film are excited / exciting, and newcomer Kristin Cox is interested / interesting as Clarkson's love interest in the movie. But the story is often confused / confusing. I didn't understand the ending at all. I was also surprised / surprising by some scenes in the film. They were very violent!

B Complete the sentences with the correct form of the words in the box.

bore confuse depress embarrass entertain surprise terrify

1. I was kind of _____ after watching that movie. It was a tearjerker!

2. I'm _____. Is our test this Friday or next Friday?

3. My film class is very _____. It's a lot of fun.

4. I watched a scary movie alone, and I was _____. It was very frightening!

5. When that movie won Best Film, it was _____. In my opinion, it was a terrible movie.

6. This movie is very _____—not interesting at all.

7. I fell asleep during class, and the teacher yelled at me. How _____!

Answer Key

Answers to page 121, Communication: Personality Quiz, Exercise B

Green	Blue	Purple	Orange
You're generous and you care about other people. You want to help them. But sometimes, you're too picky! Remember, people aren't perfect.	You're ambitious and a little bit reserved. But remember—it's important to smile. Don't be so serious all the time!	You love to learn and try new things. You're also very bright. But sometimes, you're too competitive. Let others win once in a while!	You're interesting, and you love adventure. But be careful! Sometimes you're very impulsive! Remember to think about your future, too!